Contents

You Can't Hide

Tina Renton

as told to Ruth Kelly

**SIMON &
SCHUSTER**

London · New York · Sydney · Toronto · New Delhi

A CBS COMPANY

To my amazing sons Mitchell and Daniel

First published in Great Britain by Simon & Schuster UK Ltd, 2013
A CBS COMPANY

1 3 5 7 9 10 8 6 4 2

Simon & Schuster UK Ltd
1st Floor
222 Gray's Inn Road
London WC1X 8HB

www.simonandschuster.co.uk

Simon & Schuster Australia, Sydney
Simon & Schuster India, New Delhi

A CIP catalogue record for this book
is available from the British Library.

ISBN: 978-1-84983-981-5

Typeset in Fournier by M Rules
Printed and bound by CPI Group (UK) Ltd, Croydon, CR0 4YY

While this book gives a faithful account of the author's
experiences, some names have been changed to protect
the privacy of the individuals involved.

PART ONE

Devil in Disguise

The shopping bags were so heavy I felt like my arms were going to tear out of my tiny body. I took a deep breath with every giant step up the staircase to our flat on the estate. I longed to put the bags down but I knew it would cost me.

'Oi! Take your fucking jacket with you!' Mum screamed from the car.

'I can't, my hands are full,' I pleaded, as the plastic handles dug deeper into my skin.

I jumped as I heard her slam the boot shut. She sounded like an elephant thumping up the concrete steps, huffing and puffing through her nose. Mum charged up behind me and threw the jacket at the back of my head with such force it whipped forwards across my cheeks. That strange feeling rose in my mouth, like every time I was about to have an epileptic fit. The daylight got darker and then black. And then I fell.

I woke up lying on a single bed with what looked like a shower curtain separating me from the noisy room. I could hear footsteps rushing backwards and forwards and machines bleeping. The back of my head hurt so much it felt as if someone had chopped into it like a piece of firewood. A tall man in a white coat pulled back the curtain and examined the back of my head.

'You've had a nasty fall,' he said softly. In those few words I felt more warmth and kindness than I'd ever heard spoken to me before. The doctor turned to my mum, who was slouched in the chair next to my bed. Her eyes glazed over as he explained that I needed stitches and would have to rest.

We drove home from the hospital in silence and I felt a horrible churning sensation in my stomach because I'd inconvenienced her again. I couldn't understand why I annoyed her so much; sometimes I felt like a buzzing fly she couldn't swat. This was one of those times. The pain in the back of my head vanished, as my worry for how I could make my mum like me again took over.

We snaked along the roads to our council maisonette in Maygreen Crescent in Hornchurch, Essex. The concrete high-rise dwarfed all the houses nearby. I always wondered why one floor was painted white and the next was tiled black. It looked like we were living in a giant zebra. When the neighbours hung their washing on the balcony it was like one long party streamer. I held my breath as we passed the giant bins that were always parked at the bottom of our building. I counted for five seconds more as we climbed the stairwell that stank of stale wee. I was gasping by the time Mum unlocked our front door. I went straight up to bed and let my quilt cover me like a tent. I tucked my knees into my chest and lay cuddling myself as I listened to the television blasting from downstairs. I recognised the familiar sound of *Dallas* and I could picture her slumped in her favourite spot on the sofa taking deep puffs on her cigarettes and breathing the smoke out through her nose like a dragon.

Mum could sit for hours on the sofa watching American soap operas. *Dallas* and *Dynasty* were her favourites and she got angry if I or my older brother, Blake, interrupted her. Mum didn't look anything like the glamorous women on the TV shows. She was large and always wore the same clothes whether it was sunny or snowing – a T-shirt, calf-length skirt and sandals. She had big round glasses and her chestnut hair was a shoulder-length perm. She hardly ever wore make-up or perfume, but her skin smelt of soap.

My ears pricked up from under the duvet as I heard the stairs creak. Is Mum coming up? Mum never really came to my bedroom except on Saturdays when she would inspect my room and smack me around the back of the head for not tidying properly. She didn't even tuck me into bed at night. I peeped out from under my cover to see her carrying a glass of juice. She placed it on my bedside table and then sat on the edge of my bed. Her familiar scent of soap was mixed with the horrible smell of cigarettes.

'How are you feeling?' she asked matter-of-factly. Her eyes were cold like marble balls.

My head was throbbing, my body was aching and limp from my epileptic fit, but I was so happy to have her next to me, paying me attention, that I was glad of the pain. It felt like it was only when I was sick or fought with my brother that she noticed me. I wanted to enjoy this fleeting moment, so I played up to the attention.

'I feel sick,' I mumbled pulling my lip down.

'Drink some juice and you'll be fine,' she snapped. And with that she got up and left to return to *Dallas*.

That day I cracked my head open on the step was one of my happiest childhood memories. I got special attention from Mum but usually it wasn't like that. Mum was like the controller of a spaceship, the sofa was the captain's chair, the TV remote was her joystick and Blake and I were her crew running around after her fetching her food, fags and pouring her Bacardi and Coke.

'Oi, Flossy!' she screamed up the stairs to me.

'Can you go down the shop and get me my fags,' she ordered. She'd nicknamed me Flossy because I had pink cheeks when I was born. It made me feel special. Orders were always screamed up the stairs and punishment for disobeying was a smack around my head, once with a marble rolling pin, which really hurt. Blake and I quickly worked out if we ran up to our rooms we were safe, because Mum would never move far from the sofa.

If Mum ever did a chore we would know about it.

'If you don't get down here in a fucking minute to get your washing you're grounded!'

She yelled so loudly her voice rasped. I ran from my room so quickly my little eight-year-old feet almost skied down the stairs. I scampered across the kitchen, keeping my head low to avoid Mum's blow. I didn't understand what I could do to make Mum happy, just what I did to make her hate me. I think she hated me all the time. She never cuddled me like my best friend Lisa Long's mum did with her. Lisa lived in flats nearby and her mum used to stroke her hair and hug her. I couldn't remember when Mum touched me other than to smack me.

On Friday nights Mum usually got an Indian takeaway for herself. She would open her mouth wide like a yawning cat and shovel it in like it was her last-ever meal. I didn't dare ask if I could have some, so I'd sit patiently at the other end of the sofa hoping she'd throw me a scrap. One Friday I dared to be brave – I should have known better.

'Is that nice? Can I try a bit?' I muttered, regretting my words before I'd finished my sentence.

Mum slammed her fork down and glared at me with her blue marble eyes.

'If I had shit you'd want it,' she sneered. I didn't know what she meant but I knew I'd angered her again. Her ruddy cheeks turned crimson – it was time to make myself disappear.

I made myself scarce as much as possible to keep Mum happy. School was a relief from the constant yelling at home. I was shy in the playground because I had goofy buck teeth and a short bowl haircut that made me look like a boy. I had a small group of friends who I used to play with at break times and a different group of friends near the estate who I met down the park after school. I'd sit on the swings and watch the older kids smoke and toss their fag butts into the sandpit. Some of the popular girls would drink from beer cans with the boys and I wished I could be like them. I stayed in the park for as long as possible to avoid Mum because I knew there would be a smack waiting for me for doing something wrong. As soon as I opened the front door I ran for the stairs to my room and switched on my cassette player.

I'd recorded all my favourite songs from the radio *Chart Show* onto a blank tape. The trick was to time it before the DJ started talking over the songs. Wet Wet Wet was one of my favourite groups and I could lie for hours on my bed listening to the same song. I'd sing along to cover the shouts of Mum yelling at Blake – music was the only thing that made me feel calm because it took me away to another place. I imagined the spotlight shining down on me while I sang and danced on stage. My hair was big and back-combed and my clothes sparkled just like the beautiful women on *Dynasty* and *Dallas*.

Although I had friends I often felt lonely because I had no one at home who liked me. I was convinced there must be something wrong with me for my mum to hate me so much. More than anything I wanted her to be my friend but she didn't want to be mine.

I also had an enemy in my brother Blake, which didn't make my life any easier. There were ten months between us and we would fight like cat and dog over anything and everything. I'd want to watch cartoons on ITV and he'd want to watch BBC. I'd be listening to my music and he'd turn up his stereo to drown my music out. We'd go at each other like we wanted to kill each other.

'Get out of my room!' I screamed, as Blake hovered in my doorway taunting me.

'I'm not in your room!' he yelled sarcastically, spit flying from his chubby mouth.

'Oh, for fuck's sake, you two don't have to look at each other before you start!' Mum screamed up the stairs.

It felt like I was living in a war zone but fighting with Blake was one of the only ways to get Mum's attention. By the time I was five, a smack on the head was better than being ignored.

I don't remember David Moore moving into our maisonette. I just remember him suddenly being there every day. I was five years old when he became the dad of the household in June 1980. My real dad, Michael, a greengrocer, left when I was about two. I don't remember anything about Michael except him having a massive row with my mum on the doorstep. A windowpane was smashed and then I never saw him again. Mum said he had met another woman but I thought he must have run away because he hated me.

David looked strange because he had lots of black hair swept across in a side parting and sideburns running down his face and a dimple in his chin. He had grey eyes like a stormy sky and he wore a gold chain around his neck. He was from Belfast and it sounded strange hearing my name, Tina, spoken in a Northern Irish accent. Dave was two years older than Mum – twenty-eight – and they looked like an odd couple because he was shorter than mum at five foot eight, and much skinnier. I liked him being there though because he made Mum laugh, which meant she forgot about shouting at us. They stayed up late listening to Queen and drinking. I'd creep out of bed and watch them through the banisters –

Mum would be chugging away on cigarettes while drinking Bacardi and Dave liked to swirl the ice cubes around in his Scotch between sips.

Dave fell into the role of running our household. He worked as a taxi driver in the day during the week and in the evenings he'd cook dinner and clean up while Mum watched from the sofa. She had him right under her thumb and barked orders constantly, which made me feel sorry for him. Sundays were his only day off but as soon as Dave sat down to watch TV, Mum screamed at him to hang out the washing or clean the dishes. He never fought back, which I thought was strange because my friends' dads would not let their wives speak to them like that without striking back.

Dave seemed to take his frustration out on Blake, yelling at him to tidy up, but he hardly ever raised his voice to me. Dave always tended to take my side.

On one occasion, Blake and I were watching TV, arguing.

'I want to watch BBC1!' I screamed.

'Noooo! I was here first, so I'm watching my programme,' Blake shouted, thumping my arm.

'Ooooow,' I yelped, tears welling.

'What's going on 'ere?' asked Dave, just as I was winding my arm back to punch Blake.

'I want to watch BBC1,' I sobbed.

'I was here first,' Blake snapped.

'Turn the tele over now,' Dave ordered Blake. Blake's top lip lifted into a snarl, just like the big dogs on our estate, and a smile spread across my face. Dave was my friend – finally someone in our house was looking out for me. He made me feel special because he showed me attention. He looked after me like my mum should have. He bathed me, made sure I'd brushed my teeth, and for the first time in my life I had someone tuck me into bed and switch off my light.

'Night, Flossy,' he said softly, pushing the duvet around my little body. I smelt his Old Spice aftershave as he leant over me.

'Night, Dave,' I whispered, watching him quietly close my door behind him. I fell asleep, feeling safe because Dave was looking after me now.

I could finally let down my guard when he was around. I'd built a wall of steel to protect me from Mum and Blake. I was always on alert to brace for Mum's whacks or use my fists on my brother, and I was exhausted.

I trusted Dave not to hurt me.

We didn't really do much as a family before Dave arrived, and we didn't do much after, either, but occasionally we would be treated to a day out. He took us to watch banger racing one weekend, which Blake loved. I wasn't interested in cars but that didn't matter because we were spending the day together like normal families did. I could have anything I wanted to eat and drink and Dave kept checking that I was OK. I fell asleep in the back of the car on the way home, as my legs were so tired from stomping around. We pulled up outside our maisonette but I was so exhausted I didn't want to climb the concrete stairs. I pretended to be asleep, hoping Dave would carry me up to bed. I watched him get out and then quickly shut my eyes hoping I could fool him. He opened my door and I tried not to giggle as he scooped me up in his arms. I wasn't doing a very good impression of being asleep but he seemed happy to play along and gently laid me on my bed.

Dave's approach to bathtime was much the same as everything he did in the house – something that needed to be done. I never got to splash around having fun making bubbles; it was more a case of washing me, drying me and tucking me into bed. By the time I was six I felt I was able to wash myself with a flannel but Dave always insisted he did it.

'I'll do it,' he'd say, taking it out of my hands. I folded my arms around my knees and let him scrub my neck and back. He scrubbed my chest and reached into the soapy water to wash back and forth between my legs.

One evening when Mum was watching TV downstairs, he led me into their bedroom, which was next to the bathroom. He sat on the edge of the bed like he always did when he towelled me down. I wobbled, naked, in front of him as he pulled the towel from side to side over my back. He rubbed my arms and then moved to my feet. First up and down the left leg, and then up, and up a bit further on the right leg. He didn't say a word as he cupped the towel in his hand and wiped it between my legs. He wiped again but this time I felt his fingers as well as the towel glide back and forth. It felt strange feeling his skin on my private area. I didn't like it – I thought he must have just lost his grip on the towel. He finished off with a final rub on my back.

'Now go get ready for bed,' he said, patting me on the bum, and I reached for my nightie and wriggled it over my head. I climbed into my bed and waited for Dave to tuck me in.

That night was the first of many that Dave lost his grip on the towel. His fingers would come away from the flannel in the bath and he would end up washing my privates with his hand. He liked to take his time drying me, going back and forth between my legs. I felt uneasy – I was old enough to do it myself but I trusted Dave because he'd been looking after me. I thought that's what dads did, that it was his way of showing affection. I couldn't let things go back to the way they were before he looked after me.

Mum and Dave married in November 1981, when I was six years old. It was the first time I had ever really seen my mum wear make-up. She looked pretty, with little white flowers pinning back her curly hair. She wore a dusky pink floor-length dress with a matching cardigan. I wore the same coloured dress with a white-flowered pinafore over the top and a hairband with daisies and matching white ballet shoes. I felt grown up and my aunts said I looked just like Mum, which made me happy. Dave wore a black suit with a bright red carnation in his pocket and Blake had a matching suit made up for him. Our surnames were changed to Moore, and Blake said he was going to call Dave 'Dad' now but Dave wasn't my real dad so I didn't want to.

I didn't want to do a lot of things but I was afraid of what would happen if I said no. I wanted Dave to stop washing and drying me at night. I wanted my mum to come up the stairs and tell him I was old enough to do it myself. I wanted my mum to protect me. By the time I was seven, I could reach the towel from the drying rail so he had to stop. You would have thought he'd be relieved I'd saved him the hassle every evening, but it soon became clear he missed our bath-times.

I was woken in the middle of the night to the feeling of something brushing my leg. I was coming around from a deep sleep when I felt the sensation again at the top of my thigh. My whole body stiffened as I could feel the hot breath of someone kneeling by my side. I could smell the Old Spice – it was my stepdad. *What did he want? Why wasn't he speaking?* He pulled the duvet all the way back to leave me shivering in the cold air in just my nightie. Something felt very wrong. I pretended to be asleep, hoping that would make him leave me alone. I had my back to him and my eyes were tightly shut but I could feel his face close to mine as he breathed across my cheek. He tugged on my waist, pulling me onto my back. There was a pause for a moment as I felt him breathing again and then the stroking sensation started on the top of my legs. The skin on his fingers felt rough as he brushed from the outside to the inside of my thighs. He paused again, and then pushed my nightie up to my waist. I trembled as I lay there exposed. I wanted to push my nightie back down but I couldn't let him know I was awake. He started stroking me again, but this time he wanted to touch the inside of my thighs. He brushed up and down with his fingers like he was slowly painting a fence. I could feel his fingertips sweep across my privates.

'You feel so nice,' he whispered in his Northern Irish accent.

I didn't like him speaking to me in that way, he never usually spoke like that.

'You're so lovely,' he whispered again.

I didn't react. I was pretending to be asleep.

There was another endless pause before I heard his knees creak as he rose to his feet. He tiptoed across my room, while I kept my eyes squeezed shut. The door closed and I let out a giant gasp for air – I'd been holding my breath without knowing it.

Whoosh. I froze to the sound of the toilet flush. *Was he coming back?* I listened with relief as Dave's footsteps disappeared into the bedroom he shared with my mum.

I couldn't get back to sleep for hours because my body was still frozen stiff. *What had just happened?* That horrible feeling of being alone came back like a boomerang but I had nothing to hug other than my duvet.

2

Daddy's Girl

'Don't tell your mum I bought you this,' Dave said, handing me a roll of Opal Fruits.

'All right,' I agreed, staring up at him at the supermarket checkout.

'Thanks,' I said, remembering my manners. I wasn't expecting that – Mum hardly ever bought us sweets. I didn't know why Dave was treating me. He gave me a nod as if to say we had an understanding. If I didn't tell Mum then I'd get treats.

Dave never said a word about what had happened in my room that night. He'd gone to work by the time I'd got up and everything was as normal when I came home from school that afternoon. We went shopping together on Saturday and he'd bought me sweets, which made me feel special.

I felt happy as I carried the shopping bags up the concrete steps to our flat. 'I've something you don't have, nah naaa nah nahh nahhh,' I chuckled to myself as I passed Blake in the hallway. I know something you don't know ... I smiled to myself as I passed Mum on the sofa. I rushed up to my room, sat on my bed and unwrapped the chews one after the other. Strawberry, lime, orange – I shovelled them into my mouth two at a time as if they were going to be taken out of my hands at any moment. I gathered up the wrappings and hid them in a drawer and then lay back down on my bed, buzzing from my sugar rush.

'Tina!' Mum screamed up the stairs.

'If you don't get down here in a fucking minute and help unpack the shopping . . .' she threatened.

I pulled myself up from my bed and traipsed downstairs to unload the goods.

'What makes you think it's OK to go to your room without helping unpack?' she started.

'I'm here now, aren't I?' I snapped.

'Don't you answer back to me!' Mum shrieked, raising her hand.

'Ah, leave it out, Marilyn,' Dave intervened, coming to my rescue. I'd been saved from a blow – one–nil to me. I helped put Mum's personal stash of crisps and chocolate bars in the cupboard and then I carried the toiletries up to the bathroom.

Weekends could either be quiet or like World War Three, depending on Mum's mood. If she was getting on well with Dave, then Blake and I wouldn't hear much from either of them. They spent their time smoking, chatting and drinking. If Mum had a bee in her bonnet about something then we were all in for it and I'd hide in the park until dark. During the week, Dave had time to pay me special attention. He hand-cut me skinny chips for dinner. I was allowed to sit in the front of the car, which drove Blake mad with jealousy.

But I was the one who had to endure the visits in the night.

I didn't hear Dave come in after his taxi shift – I was always in bed by 8 p.m. It felt like the middle of the night again when I was woken by a rough hand stroking the small of my back. A chill bolted down my spine. I froze as the hand travelled to the backs of my legs and then tugged on my hips to roll me over. Again, I played dead, like a frightened animal trying to stay alive. I let my body flop onto my back and waited for what was next – I knew it wasn't over yet. On the outside I was asleep, on the inside every muscle was pulled taut. I smelt cigarettes and Old Spice as he leant over and scrunched my nightie up to my waist. He ran his hand up my thigh, higher, and higher. My head was still facing away from him, my eyes screwed tightly shut. I buried my face into my giant teddy bear as his fingers brushed where they shouldn't, backwards and forwards.

'You feel so nice,' he whispered. I squirmed inside – he was speaking in that funny voice again.

I smelt his stale breath on my face and then I was jolted by a tug on my pants. Then another tug – left and right, as he struggled to wriggle them down. I could feel their elastic tight around my knees, binding me to the bed. *Why did he want my pants off?* I was embarrassed knowing he was staring at my private parts. He started brushing my legs again and then I felt his fingers slip between them and run back and forwards on my skin. I could feel his breath across my stomach as if he was watching his hand closely.

'Do you like that?' he asked, like he expected me to answer. I buried my head deeper into the fur of my teddy bear. Dave leant across me and pulled the bear away. I had to try my hardest to act like I hadn't noticed – because I was asleep. *Give me back my bear!* I screamed inside. I felt its fur on my leg. *What was he doing with my bear? Put my bear back, he's my friend.*

I felt something soft and furry between my legs.

'You should touch yourself,' Dave whispered again, stroking me with the fur. *What does he mean, touch myself? What is he doing with my bear? Why is he speaking to me in his funny voice?*

'You should feel what it feels like to touch yourself,' he said again, stroking the furry paw up and down. I wanted him to stop. I didn't like my bear touching my private area. His breathing got faster like he was getting excited and then it slowed down again. Just like last time, he suddenly got up and left. *Had I done something wrong?* I felt so confused. I stayed like a statue until I heard him back in Mum's room, and then I pulled my knickers up and clutched my bear back by my side, where he belonged.

'I'm sorry,' I whispered, hugging him and kissing his nose. I don't know when I finally got back to sleep but I was startled awake by Dave yelling at Blake.

'Get out of bed, you fucking cunt!' he shouted down the corridor. I could hear him charging towards Blake's room like a rhino. Dave was turning more into a Michelin Man every day – I could imagine his short, stocky broad-shouldered body ramming down the door. I jumped as the door smacked open against Blake's wall.

'Up!' he yelled again. He must have been only centimetres from Blake's face.

'In a minute,' Blake whined. Blake had never been good at getting up for school.

'Get . . .' SMACK. 'Out . . .' SMACK. 'Of fucking bed . . .' SMACK SMACK. 'Now.' SMACK.

I winced as I heard Dave's fist pummel into Blake for the final time. He kicked Blake's door open and marched back downstairs. I hated Blake, but I felt sorry for him, because that must have hurt like hell. I craned my ear to hear if he was still moving. There was a rustling noise, so I pulled my door ajar to peek. Blake limped to the bathroom in just his pants; his back had half-a-dozen red marks imprinted across it.

I threw on my uniform, terrified Dave would do the same to me. I didn't know what my stepdad was capable of any more. I didn't like what he did to me in the night but I didn't want to be beaten. I crept down for breakfast – embarrassed and afraid at the same time. Dave was busy thrashing about in the cupboards trying to find something, so I quietly climbed up onto a chair at the table. My legs still weren't long enough for my feet to touch the ground.

'What do you want to eat? Cereal?' Dave growled.

'Yes, please,' I said. I was too shy to look at him.

'Here you are,' he said, sloshing a bowl of cornflakes and milk under my nose. He was acting like nothing had happened. *So maybe this is just what all dads do with their eight-year-old daughters? Maybe it's OK?* He must like me more than Blake though. At least someone likes me, I thought and smiled.

Mum came trudging down the stairs, wrapping her dressing gown around her curves.

'Why aren't you ready yet?' she barked. 'You're as bad as your brother.'

I stared into my cereal bowl.

'Got any fags?' she asked Dave.

'No, I'll go down the shop when I get back from dropping the kids off,' he said.

She grunted with irritation, then stomped back upstairs to bed.

I didn't talk to any of my friends at school about what my dad liked to do to me in the middle of the night – I was too embarrassed. Dave's visits became regular, twice a week, usually after he'd finished a late shift – he liked to say goodnight to me before going to bed. I always pretended to be asleep but he always spoke to me like we were having a conversation. He'd started to slip the tip of his finger inside me. I really hated that because it made me feel sore in class the next day. I wanted him to stop but I was scared of him and I was confused because he kept doing nice things for me. The past few weekends he'd bought me sweets on our shopping trips, so I could be like all the other girls at school.

'Don't tell your mum I've got you this,' Dave said, grabbing a hair mousse off the beauty shelf. He looked nervously, left to right down the aisle, as he placed it in the cardboard box in our shopping trolley. I couldn't understand why he was making such a fuss of packing it away, so I stood on my tiptoes and peered over to get a closer look. Dave had created a false bottom in the box by putting one box inside another. I watched as he hid my present in the secret compartment.

'Shhh,' he said, winking at me.

'What else would you like?'

I stared up at him in disbelief. He was shoplifting.

Mum had told us stealing was naughty and what all the bad kids on the estate did, and we would be arrested if we did it too. *But how bad could it be if Dave was doing it?* I looked longingly at the make-up, I'd never tried make-up before, let alone own my own.

'Do you want some make-up?' Dave asked.

I nodded with excitement. I reached up and picked a bright blue eye shadow, just like the popular girls wore, and handed it to him.

'Don't tell your mum,' he said again, and slipped it into the secret box. My heart was pounding as we walked to the checkout, but Dave was calm, his face gave nothing away. I kept looking up at him for reassurance but he stared ahead as he unpacked our groceries onto the conveyor belt. I was scared but excited at the same time – I was his accomplice just like in the movies. I held my breath until he had handed over the cash and then let out a massive sigh of relief. Then came the rush – I had hair mousse and eye shadow; everyone was going to be jealous of me.

'You take these straight up to your room,' Dave warned, pointing his finger at me.

I understood – if I was a good girl and kept quiet, I would get presents. Dave had made sure he'd packed all the toiletries in one bag, which I was responsible for taking up to the bathroom. I carried them up as soon as we were through the door.

'What's got into her?' Mum sneered at my helpfulness.

I didn't wait for her follow-up snipe; I was already grabbing my presents and hiding them in my wardrobe. I went to bed that night feeling like I'd had a good day.

Five hours later, I was awake. I didn't want to be, but my stepdad was back in my room. Hopefully it wouldn't last long this time, I prayed, as I smelt the Scotch on his breath. He rolled me straight onto my back this time and was touching me harder than usual. I didn't like it, I wanted him to stop. I smelt him move his face close to mine and then his rough hands grabbed my jaw, as he pulled me towards his lips. He pressed down hard on me as he tried to force his tongue inside my mouth. It was horrible, like a giant slug wriggling around. I pushed my head back so deep into my pillow I felt like I was going to go through the mattress.

My eyes were now half open. I saw him for the first time – my stepdad – naked with just his white pants around his ankles. I wriggled free and turned my back so far away he could barely see my face. I couldn't stop gasping for air. I could feel his eyes watching me and I wanted to be sick. I did what I knew best – pretended I was asleep. I don't know how long he sat by my side, but I knew the whole time there was much more to come.

He waited until my breathing calmed and then he tugged at my waist again. He pulled my knickers off and stroked between my legs.

'Tsk,' I heard him tut with irritation as I'd deliberately

pressed my knees together. He got up and walked to the door. I couldn't believe it, pretending I was asleep had worked; he was going to leave me alone tonight. But why hasn't he closed it behind him? My body stiffened as I realised there was a change in the ritual. I heard him rummage around in the bathroom and walk back into my bedroom and close the door behind him. He knelt beside me and then I heard a lid being unscrewed. It was like feeling my way through the dark – I could only guess what was about to happen to me from the noises – and I was terrified.

I felt something cold and gooey on my thigh. It was horrible and he was spreading it with his fingers. He massaged the cold creamy substance over my inner thighs, prising my legs apart.

'That feels nice, doesn't it?' he asked.

I wanted to scream, *No!*

He forced his fingers between my legs and flicked them quickly.

'Do you like it when I touch you here?' he whispered.

No no no, I whimpered inside. Stop talking to me.

His voice had become breathless and I could hear a strange noise like he was pulling at something on his body. He slipped his finger inside me, all the way in, it really hurt. I had to try so hard to pretend I was asleep as it burnt inside. The rubbing noise got louder and faster and Dave was groaning. I tried to block out the pain by telling myself it would be over soon. He let out a grunt and the noise stopped. He pulled his finger out of me and got up and left.

I pulled the covers back over me and rubbed my knees together to ease the soreness.

I woke up in the morning with the strange feeling I'd got used to having now – like I'd had a bad dream that was painfully real. And I did the same thing I'd got used to doing – swept it to the back of my mind. The one person – my mum – who I should have been able to talk to about it, was the last person on earth I could tell. I didn't share anything with her, not even a mouthful of her curry on Friday nights. And if I told her, then my treats from Dave would stop, and I would be beaten like Blake. I rationalised Dave's behaviour like the shoplifting – if a grown-up is doing it, how bad can it be? Grown-ups are clever and do the right thing.

I peeled myself out of bed and tiptoed to the bathroom, hoping I wouldn't bump into Dave.

'Ouch,' I whimpered as I went for a pee. It was sore like someone had scratched me down there. I crossed my arms around my stomach and rocked forward to ease the pain.

'Oi, is that you in there, Flossy?' Mum yelled.

'Yes,' I bleated, prising myself off the toilet seat.

'Get a fucking move on, I need to go,' she ordered.

I threw my imaginary armour back on and got on with it. That was the only way to survive in our family.

'About bloody time,' Mum sneered, as I limped back to my room.

'Make yourself useful and bring Dave and me a cup of tea and coffee,' she said.

I did a U-turn and headed down the stairs to put on the kettle. I suddenly felt exposed, standing there in my nightie, so I folded my arms across my chest. I hated the way I looked – I'm fat and ugly with sticky-out teeth. *Is that why my mum doesn't like me?* Tears welled in my eyes and the painful reminder of last night vanished, as all I could think about was how disgusting I was. At least Dave likes me, I sobbed. That's better than being hated. That's better than being alone.

3

Someone to Love

When Dave wasn't touching me, I never thought about it. They were uncomfortable memories that got washed down the plughole like the bath water. It didn't enter my head whether or not he'd carry on giving me special goodnights when we went on summer holiday to Highfield Holiday Park in Clacton-on-Sea. Life was enough of a struggle as it was – if I stopped to think about what was happening to me I'd make chinks in my armour. I'd even taught myself not to cry, to make me stronger. I'd think angry thoughts about my brother or my mum to stop the tears falling when the prickle feeling started in my eyes.

There was nothing glamorous about Highfields, but for us it was a real treat to stay in a caravan for a week. All four of us were squished into a tiny rectangle, which had a double bed and two bunk beds and a kitchen. The bathroom was a concrete building across the campsite, which stank of mouldy towels and bleach. Mum loved taking us to Highfields because she could leave Blake and me to look after ourselves and spend the rest of the day eating and drinking with Dave. Anything that took us off her hands seemed to make her happy.

I loved the pool best of all because I rarely got to swim. Blake liked to pretend he was Jaws the shark and pull me underwater. I couldn't bear not being able to breathe, as it reminded me of when Dave tried to kiss me. The only way to survive was to fight back and I bit him so hard in the arm I nearly drew blood.

'Arrrrgh, get the fuck off me!' Blake screamed, splashing water in my eyes.

'You get off me!' I yelled back, coughing and spluttering. Was there nowhere I could have peace? I swam towards the side of the pool, where Mum had parked herself on a sun-lounger. She was sprawled out on the white plastic chair in her flowery swimming costume that showed off her cleavage and her belly. She was reading a women's magazine while Dave was queuing at the bar.

'Mum, Blake tried to drown me,' I whined, trying to get her attention.

'Oh, for fuck's sake,' she muttered, not even lifting her eyes from her magazine.

I wasn't going to give up and I tried another tactic to get her to look at me.

'Mum, I can swim a length underwater,' I boasted.

'Go on then, show me,' she said. My plan had worked. I was determined to show her I could do something right, so I dragged myself to the end of the pool to begin my challenge. 'One, two three,' I said, before taking a big gulp of air and plunging my head under. I wasn't a strong swimmer but I did my best breaststroke underwater to get me to the other end. The chlorine burnt my eyes and my lungs were heaving for

air but I kept going, and going, until I could see the shallow
end in sight. I rose out of the water like a fountain, gasping.
I looked over to Mum but she was shovelling chips into her
mouth and laughing with Dave. She hadn't noticed me. I was
so exhausted I wanted to cry but I held it in – I didn't want
her to see I was upset.

I climbed out by the metal steps and quickly ran for my
towel. I wrapped it around myself so no one could see my
body. I headed over to Mum and Dave but they still hadn't
noticed me, so I took myself away to a sunlounger and put
a towel over my head so I could disappear until dinner time.

Dave cooked as usual and Blake and I were allowed to go
to the clubhouse until bedtime. I could hear Mum giggling
and I wondered what Dave said to her to make her so happy.
I turned over, wishing I had my big teddy bear to cuddle me
to sleep.

I woke in the middle of the night to hear something creaking. I froze and automatically played dead, expecting the
hand on my back at any moment. I waited, and waited, my
heart pounding – but nothing. I slowly turned over to have
a peek but my stepdad wasn't in the room. All I could hear
was Blake's heavy breathing. I was wide awake now and
needed the toilet, which was horrible because I'd have to run
across the campsite to the smelly concrete bathroom. I lay
there for as long as I could, holding it in, but eventually I
dragged myself up and out. I tiptoed past the kitchen and ran
across the grass in my bare feet as fast as I could, using the
light of the moon to guide me. The bright strip light in the
women's shower block flickered, making the room spookier

than it already was. There were some names scrawled over the back of the toilet door and I kept imagining shadows coming underneath the cubicle.

As soon as I was done, I sprinted back, reached up to the caravan door, and pulled. *Why isn't it opening?* I pushed the handle down again but it wouldn't budge. No, please, no . . . My heart sank as I realised I'd locked myself out. There was no way I was going to wake my mum up and get a scolding. I'd rather sit in the cold all night than make her hate me even more. I slid down the door and landed in a heap on the caravan step. I tugged my nightie over my knees to cover my bare legs, wrapped my arms around my ankles and tucked my head into my thighs like I'd seen the ducks do on the lake. I managed to drop off to sleep for a bit but my shivers kept waking me up. The night used to be the only time I would find peace but it had turned into my enemy. The tweeting birds were my only comfort, as I counted the minutes until breakfast when I could knock on the door and be let in. As soon as I heard a noise inside I started banging.

'What the hell are you doing out there?' Dave asked.

'I got locked out,' I said, my lips trembling with cold.

'Get in here,' he said, helping lift me to my feet.

'What's happened?' Mum shouted from her bed.

'Tina locked herself out all night,' he explained.

'Dozy bitch,' Mum cackled.

Blake roared with laughter and I flashed him a sarcastic smile. I was too tired and too cold to fight back and it was easier to be laughed at.

When Dave announced that Mum was having a baby, I

was so happy because I'd finally have a friend. I assumed it would be a girl and I'd look after her and, when she was older, we'd share clothes and make-up. I'd finally have someone to talk to and tell my secrets to. I can't remember anything about the pregnancy, what Mum looked like or how she was with us; the first memory is of Dave driving us to the hospital.

'Have you seen her already? What's she like? Will I be able to hold her?' I asked Dave, who seemed flustered behind the wheel.

'We're nearly there,' he cut me short.

'Your mum's exhausted, so I don't want you two fighting. Is that understood?' he said, looking in the rear-view mirror at Blake. 'No trouble from you, you little cunt,' he spat at him.

'Why are you always having a go at me?' Blake snapped.

I zoned out from the shouting, as I was too excited about meeting my new little friend. I bounded out of the front seat and balanced along the kerbstones like it was a tightrope while I waited for Dave to pay for parking. I couldn't remember the last time I had so much energy except for when I was running from Mum's slaps.

We followed Dave through the long corridors that seemed to go on for miles. The floor made squeaky noises under our trainers and the place stank of antiseptic. All the adults dressed in white and blue gowns looked harassed, like they should have already been somewhere ten minutes ago. Wheelchairs and beds overtook us like we were on a busy motorway. As we turned into the maternity ward, the sound of babies crying got me even more excited.

'Wait 'ere,' Dave ordered, as he poked his nose into Mum's cubicle to check she was ready for us. He signalled us in and I pushed forward to beat Blake to the post. Mum was sitting up in bed; her cheeks were more ruddy than usual and her hair was messy and greasy and had been clipped back. Beside her was a cot with my baby sister inside. I stood on my tiptoes and peered in.

'Hi, I'm Tina,' I whispered, reaching for her tiny hand with my pinky finger.

'Meet your baby brother, Jonathan,' Mum beamed.

'What, it's a boy?' I stuttered with confusion. No one had mentioned the sex of the baby but I'd assumed I had a sister simply because I wanted one so badly. I didn't want another horrible brother like Blake; I needed a sister who would be my friend. I felt the tears prickle behind my eyes and I conjured up angry thoughts. I threw myself down in the chair next to Mum and crossed my arms.

'I wanted a sister,' I said, kicking my feet.

'Well unfortunately you don't get to choose,' Mum said sarcastically.

Mum must have thought I was being a brat but it was my way of hiding my sadness. I'd pinned all my hopes on a sister changing my life and I didn't realise until that moment how unhappy I really was.

'Do you want to hold him?' Mum asked.

'No,' I said, sulking.

'Fine, be like that,' Mum said, dismissing me.

I was nearly ten when Jonathan joined our family in 1985. He slept in a cot in Mum and Dave's room and, after I had got over the initial disappointment, I was all over my baby brother. I wanted to help change his nappies; if he cried I'd go running to him. I wanted to play with him and hold him all the time. I loved looking after him because he made me feel grown up and, best of all, he made me feel needed.

Mum quickly latched on to the fact that I liked to do baby chores and gladly handed them over. Sitting on Mum's bed holding Jonathan in my arms, feeling his tiny warm body against mine, was one of my happiest childhood memories.

'Whhhhhaaaaa!' he screamed.

'Shhh, I'm here now,' I hushed him, rocking him gently in my arms. Within seconds he had stopped crying.

'See, you like me, don't you?' I whispered, nuzzling into his face with my nose. He took me away from the anger and fighting of downstairs. When I was with Jonathan, however fleeting the moment, I was transported to a happy place where people loved each other.

'You'll be my friend for ever, won't you?' I said, holding his hand with my little finger. His friendly baby smile beamed back at me.

'I'll protect you,' I promised. It was only a silly child's promise but somewhere inside I meant it. I believed he needed my protection.

But just when I thought my life was finally getting better, it suddenly turned much worse. By the age of ten I was more developed than all the other girls in my class – I'd sprouted breasts and I was taller and bigger than my friends. I hated PE because I couldn't bear anyone seeing my body. I didn't know why my body was changing – my mum never sat me down and had a chat about the birds and the bees. I thought I was a freak, and my weird body was yet another reason for my mum to hate me. But the worst thing about developing breasts was that my stepdad spent longer in my bedroom at night.

I don't know how I managed to fall asleep, never knowing whether Dave would be coming in. There was no pattern to the nights he chose; just that it was always late, after Mum had gone to bed. My ability to not think about it when it wasn't happening was working. It was much harder to get to sleep afterwards, though, because of the stinging feeling.

'Have you touched yourself yet?' whispered Dave, as he knelt by my bed.

He pulled back the duvet to find me sleeping in my pyjamas. I'd started wearing them every night now because I'd worked out it would slow my stepdad down. I didn't let Mum wash them for fear I wouldn't have them back by the evening.

'Humph,' Dave sighed, as he was forced to pull down my pyjamas and my pants whilst I pretended to be a dead weight.

'Argh, you don't make it easy,' he grumbled.

He'd come prepared with his pot of greasy cold stuff again. The sound of the lid being unscrewed triggered my body to stiffen. He smelt of alcohol tonight. That meant the stinging feeling afterwards would be worse. I built another layer on my protective wall as I prepared myself for the worst.

'Kiss me,' he demanded. I could feel specks of his spit

over my face. He'd never tried to kiss me again after that night, but he kept asking. Dave wasn't one to give up when he wanted something and he wanted me twice a week. I didn't answer, as usual, so he kept going. He lifted up my top to reveal my little breasts. He cupped them roughly with his hands and massaged my nipples.

'You feel so nice,' he drooled.

He circled around and around and then he leant forward. I felt something slimy and wet and warm on my skin. He couldn't kiss my lips so he was now kissing my breasts. *Stop, stop, it feels horrible.*

'You liked that, didn't you?' he whispered.

He tugged my legs apart and then did the same down there. Of all the things he did I hated that most of all – his horrible slimy, stinking mouth on my private parts. He grabbed my limp hand and shoved it between his legs, placing it on his penis. But it wasn't like I knew a penis to be – it was hard and big. I was still pretending to be asleep, so my hand fell down, hitting the side of the bed. He grabbed my wrist roughly and wrapped it around his penis. It was horrible and wet and I didn't know what he wanted from me. He cupped his hand around mine and started moving it back and forwards, which made him make those funny grunting noises again. He tightened his grip as he moved my hand more vigorously, up and down, up and down, so hard it was making my whole arm ache. It seemed like it lasted for an hour before he let out that really big grunting noise. He then got up and walked to my bedroom door. I did something I hadn't dared do before – I opened my eyes to check he was really leaving. His stocky body was naked except for a pair of small pants. Even in the dark I could see the shadow of his belly on the wall. I closed my eyes again as he pulled the door to, just in case he caught me peeking.

I couldn't get to sleep that night. My aching arm kept reminding me of his visit. I did my best to keep my armour on but no matter how many angry thoughts I conjured up I couldn't stop the prickles in the back of my eyes. I wrapped myself up so tightly in my duvet I felt as if I was in an oven. I didn't want anyone else getting inside it with me. I didn't make any noise when I cried. I sobbed silent tears into my pillow and rocked myself to a calmer place.

Was I to blame for my stepdad wanting to touch me because my body was different to all the other girls my age? I really hated my reflection in the mirror now and, no matter how many hair mousses and lipsticks Dave bought me, I couldn't bear to look at myself. I'd get out of the bath and stare at all my horrible wobbly bits and make a little prayer that one day I'd turn into a swan. I don't know why I bothered though . . . I'd stopped believing in fairy tales a long time ago because I was forced to grow up so quickly.

'I hate you,' I spat at my reflection. I wanted to punch myself, I felt so angry.

I'd become even more shy around my friends at school. I felt like I was the thorn between the roses, and by keeping my mouth shut I wouldn't draw attention to myself. I wanted my mum to be the one to reassure me I wasn't hideous. She never told me I was pretty, so I had tantrums to try to prise it out of her.

'Mum, do you think all my friends are prettier than me?' I asked her as she put Jonathan to bed.

'Don't be stupid, Flossy,' she sighed with irritation.

'They are. I'm the ugly one who no one likes,' I whined. *Look up, look at me, I wanted to scream at her*. She was my mum and I wanted her to reassure me I was OK and not the monster I thought I was. I wanted her to tell me she loved me.

Instead she said nothing, and carried on as if I wasn't in the room. I was Invisible Tina again, who needed to scream to get her attention.

'I AM UGLY!' I shouted. And then burst into tears.

'For fuck's sake, I've just put Jonathan to bed,' she hissed. 'Wind it in, for God's sake. You can't change who you are, you just got to get on with it. It's the same for everyone. Not everyone can be a supermodel,' was her answer. It was Mum's whole attitude to life – shut up and get on with it.

I carried on sobbing, hoping she would take pity on me and wrap her arms around my little shoulders, but she walked out without looking back and returned to her beloved TV. I no longer had an audience but I couldn't stop the tears rolling down my rosy cheeks. I cried so hard I stopped making a noise and was left wheezing for air. 'Mum's going to kill me. I've made her quilt all wet,' I heaved, trying to soak it up with the sleeve of my jumper.

'You still love me, don't you?' I asked Jonathan, who had slept through the whole drama.

'It's OK, I know you do.' I smiled between my sniffles.

'Come on, Tina, buck up!' I shouted at myself. Crying made me feel weak and vulnerable because it reminded me of the times when I was most upset. It reminded me of my stepdad in my room. I forced myself off the bed and went back to my room to listen to my music tapes.

My new breasts were just the start of my horrible body changes. I wish my mum had warned me what was to follow, as I was caught out on one of my shopping trips with Dave. He was filling up his cardboard box with goodies for me when I had an urgent sensation for the loo. I dashed off to the store toilets and unzipped my white jeans to find a pool of blood spreading across the fabric. I wobbled back onto the toilet seat. I was so shocked. What's happening to me? I grabbed a piece of loo roll and wiped between my legs – more blood. My heart raced as I panicked. Oh, my God, am I going to bleed to death? Suddenly the cool toilet cubicle turned into a sauna, as I started to burn up. Beads of sweat collected on my back and chest, my palms were glistening with sweat. I needed to get help, but the thought of walking back into the store with bloodstained white jeans was mortifying. I sponged some toilet roll into my trousers, desperately hoping that would soak some of it up.

'Oh, my God, oh, my God,' I repeated. I hated anyone looking at me but now everyone would be staring. I sat paralysed on the toilet seat, too frightened to move. It seemed like someone up above had it in for me and I just didn't know how much longer I could hold on.

'Get up, Tina, MOVE!' The fighter inside blossomed out from my despair. I peeled myself from the seat and winced as I pulled my soggy jeans up. I slid open the lock and hesitantly walked for the door.

'One two three, go,' I said, pulling back the door into the bustling supermarket. I wrapped my arms across my chest and put my head down as I began the search for my stepdad – the man who may have caused me to bleed. I didn't know what was happening, or if his touching had damaged me. We never talked about what he liked to do to me, so I dreaded telling him there was something wrong with me down there. I zigzagged my way up and down the aisles; I thought everyone was staring at me and my big red stain.

Where are you? I felt like I was going to have a panic attack. I kept walking, arms folded, head down. He would have to be in the very last aisle with the booze. I sighed, as I finally set eyes on him.

'Where the fuck have you been?' Dave snapped.

I shuffled up to him. I couldn't bear to look down to see if the stain had spread even further. I felt so humiliated.

'I'm bleeding,' I mumbled. 'Down there,' I said, pointing. My cheeks were burning red with embarrassment.

'I'll go get you some things,' he said matter-of-factly. 'Go sit in the car,' he ordered, handing me the keys.

I nodded and walked as quickly as I could to the car park. What did he mean, get me some things? What's wrong with my stupid body? What did he know that I didn't? I felt the prickles attacking my eyes as I sat alone in the car. It seemed like for ever before he returned. We sat in silence for the drive home – he looked deep in thought as he snaked through the neighbouring estates.

I carried in the bags and waited for someone to tell me if I was dying. Dave muttered something to Mum and she walked over to me with a box in her hand.

'What's wrong with me?' I whimpered.

'You're having a period. It happens once a month. You have to put this in your pants,' she said, handing me a sanitary towel. She turned back to the shopping bags. She was much more interested in finding her crisps.

So I wasn't bleeding to death then. I stood at the bottom of the stairs, holding the pad box, feeling a mixture of relief and anger that my mum couldn't give me five seconds of her time. I still didn't really understand what was happening to me; it was just a case of finding out for myself.

I was yet to find out that my period was a blessing in disguise. The one body change that I could use to protect me from my stepdad.

4

House of Horrors

By my final year of primary school, I had hardly any friends left because of my fading confidence. I was rarely asked to friends' houses to play, so when I was invited to a birthday party one Saturday afternoon I was over the moon. *Someone likes me.* I beamed from ear to ear when I opened the invitation. Some of the popular kids would be there and we would be getting cake and take-home party bags. Best of all, I'd be away from my family for most of the day. I asked Mum to help me pick out a party outfit because I had nothing to wear. I asked if I could have a new top but she said I had to be fucking joking. I asked her to help me look pretty, but she couldn't be bothered to come to my room to help me choose from what I had. I was so desperate to have friends that I turned to Dave for help – knowing it was going to cost me.

'Could I have that and that?' I asked, picking off a green eye shadow and pink lipstick from the supermarket shelf. 'I've got a birthday party to go to.' I smiled proudly. I needed to look pretty so the girls would like me.

'Go on then.' He winked.

Tina Renton

Even though Jonathan was his own son, his own blood, Dave still treated me like his favourite and I liked being put first by someone. I was that desperate for affection.

It was a good thing that I had picked out my make-up, as our usual Saturday-morning shopping trip had to be scrapped because we were taken to our grandparents' house on the Friday night before the party. It wasn't to my mum's mum who lived up the road, but to Rose and Wally, my real dad's mum. It had been so long since I'd met them, I didn't have a clue who they were when we pulled up outside their house. Blake and I were dropped off on the Friday night without any explanation.

'Where are we?' I mumbled.

'At your Nan, Rose's,' Mum said matter-of-factly.

'Why are we here?' I whined.

No answer. Mum got out and greeted Rose and Wally in the drive, while Dave unloaded our weekend rucksacks and handed them to Wally.

'You remember Rose and Wally, don't you?' Mum said, shoving me forward into their arms.

'Hi,' I mumbled. I was always shy around new people and Rose and Wally might as well have been strangers.

Blake brazenly stomped into their house and made himself at home on the sofa, demanding to watch the TV. Their house was like taking a time machine back to the 1960s. The living room was covered in brown carpet with big orange and yellow flowers. The kitchen was really strange, with copper walls – I'd never seen anything like it.

'Are you hungry?' Nan asked.

I nodded shyly. Nan seemed nice. She had a warmth and kindness about her that I rarely got to experience. I felt like she was going to look after me and I was safe. I was allowed seconds for supper and we were also treated to a pudding, and I fell asleep bloated but happy on the sofa, dreaming of my party the next day.

I woke bolt upright in the middle of the night not knowing where I was. It took a few minutes to calm down and get my bearings. I reached my hand around to the back of my neck – it was dripping with sweat. I felt feverish and dizzy and I slumped back onto my pillow. I woke up early the next morning, feeling even worse. Nan popped her head around the door to find me curled up, groaning.

'What's wrong, love?' she said, feeling my forehead.

'You're burning up,' she exclaimed.

'I'm OK,' I coughed and spluttered.

'Your mum told me about your party; you can't go if you feel this ill,' she said sympathetically.

'No, I want to go,' I demanded, tears filling my eyes. 'Pleeease,' I begged. I needed to go; it was one of the few parties I'd ever been invited to.

'No, sweetheart, you need to rest,' she insisted.

'Noooooo,' I cried, rolling over. *Why me? Why always me?* I scrunched my duvet into my face and cried silent tears. My body had let me down, again.

Nan was extra nice to me that day, and by dinner on Sunday I was feeling better. I hadn't missed home one bit and I didn't ask when I was going back. I helped Nan cook dinner, which was a real treat because I'd never done that before. I felt like I was needed and I pretended I was on a cooking show by preparing neat piles of vegetables to be thrown into the pan. *I wish Mum would do this with me.* I asked if I could wash up too, because I loved the feeling of helping out and being like a grown-up.

'Come on, then, let's take you home,' Nan said, as I put the last dish away. Blake was back in front of the TV, and both of us were happy to stay where we were. We reluctantly hopped in the back of the car with our bags on our knees, and Grandad drove us home to our maisonette.

'We're going to stop in at some friends on the way,' Nan said, looking back at us. We nodded, happy at any delay to the journey home. A couple of miles later, they pulled up outside a semi-detached red-brick house with a paved drive-way. We followed behind Nan and Grandad as they led us up the path to the front door, which was already ajar.

'Hello?' Grandad shouted as we stepped inside.

A little boy with blond hair, wearing a bright all-in-one suit, was standing in the hallway.

'Oh, my brother Jonathan's got one of those outfits,' I said, as we walked into the large living room, which had a sofa and chairs just like in our maisonette. It also had the same TV and the same pictures on the wall. *Hang on a minute, everything in the house was the same as in our flat.* And there was Mum and Dave standing in the dining room.

'Thanks for looking after them,' Mum said to Nan.

What was happening? Where were we? Where were all my things? I felt my heart race as that familiar feeling of panic set in. There were no boxes, no sign of any house move, it

was like someone had sucked all our things out of our flat
and put them in this strange house in the space of a weekend.

'Mum, where am I?' I asked, totally confused.

'In our new house,' she said, walking off.

And that was all the explanation I got. That horrible feeling of being alone hit me like a truck as I stood by myself in
the massive living room. I was so confused by it all, I hadn't
even recognised my own brother Jonathan when I walked in.

'Where's my bedroom? Where are all my things?' I panicked. I was informed I had the small single room opposite
the bathroom. I felt like I was living a dream as I made my
way upstairs – walking through a strange house that looked
like we'd lived in it for ten years. I'd grown to hate surprises,
thanks to never knowing what would happen in the night, so
I cautiously edged my way into my new bedroom. I was
expecting something to jump out at me any minute like they
do in the scary movies. I couldn't believe it, my room was
identically laid out. My bed was along the left-hand wall, my
wardrobe opposite, my toys on the shelves with my tapes
neatly lined in a row. And there was big bear on my blanket.
I stood on my tiptoes and peered out of the window to see
a view of the street, which curved into a horseshoe. Maybe
this isn't so bad after all. I smiled. I'd never lived in a house
before and we even had a garden to play in. I ran back downstairs, bursting with excitement. Mum and Dave were
laughing and looked happy.

'Like yer room, eh?' Dave said. 'You can decide how you
want it decorated,' he added, grinning at the idea of spoiling
me again.

'I want it flick-painted with lots of different colours like blues and yellows and reds.' I giggled.

This was going to be a new beginning. Mum and Dave looked happy, so maybe Mum would love me too now? Maybe now I had a new room and Dave wouldn't be able to touch me in the night? I pinched myself, just to make sure this wasn't a dream.

Our new house was modern and on a council estate called Montgomery Crescent, Harold Hill, about eight miles from our previous flat. I had no idea why we moved – questions like that didn't get asked in our family, but I wondered if it had something to do with Mum having screaming matches with the neighbours.

'You'll have a new school to go to on Monday,' Mum announced.

What? I only had a few more months left at my primary school. What's she talking about?

'I don't understand,' I said, my lip quivering.

'We've moved, so you're moving school,' Mum snapped.

'But what about my friends?' I gasped.

Again there was no explanation. There was no sympathetic, 'Don't worry, you'll still be able to see your friends.' There was nothing.

'But I didn't get to go to the party. I didn't get to say goodbye,' I pleaded.

Mum just shrugged her shoulders. I let out a howl of anger, stomped to my new bedroom and dived under my quilt. Although I'd never had the courage to tell my friends what Dave was doing to me, they were still a comfort. It was back to being all alone. No friends. No escape.

BANG! I thumped the wall so hard with my fist it went numb.

My ability to stop myself from crying wasn't working any more. Tears ran down my cheeks and bled into my pillow. If only I had gone to the party, I could have kept my friends.

In my heart I knew our new house wasn't a fresh start at all, that my stepdad was still going to come into my room, because I still took extra precautions before going to bed. I wore my PJs and a pair of knickers, hoping that would make him leave me alone.

On one occasion, Mum and Dave had gone out for the evening, so Mum's brother Tony and his girlfriend Nicky looked after us. I tried to fall asleep but my tummy had been grumbling, so I snuck down to the kitchen to see what I could forage. The TV was blaring; the coast was clear to open the fridge. My eyes grew big as saucers when I spotted a slab of cheese on the back shelf. I looked over my shoulder to check Uncle Tony wasn't in the kitchen, and grabbed it.

'Put it back,' Tony said, and smirked. 'C'mon, you've had dinner, off to bed,' he ordered. I pulled a sulky face and traipsed back upstairs, annoyed at myself for not being quiet enough.

I woke to the smell of Old Spice, cigarettes and alcohol wafting over me. It must have been really late because I felt like I'd been asleep for a long time. I was in an almost comatose state as Dave yanked my quilt off me and flung it to the end of the bed. I quickly became wide awake as he struggled with my pyjamas and knickers. I felt his nails dig into my skin as he yanked my clothes over my bum. He was quick to not let my legs flop closed and grabbed them with his rough hands, pushing them apart. There was no need for his creams tonight – he already had me like he wanted me.

He started talking to me again. He was very persistent about asking me to touch myself.

'Have you tried touching yourself?' he whispered with his fingers inside me. 'You should try touching yourself here,' he drooled, moving his finger from left to right as if he was giving me a lesson.

'If you do it like this, you'll really enjoy it.' He went on like he was having a conversation with me.

He slipped his finger inside me and wriggled it around and then he thrust more fingers in me. I don't know how many he used but it was so painful I had to call on my strength not to make a sound.

You're asleep, you're asleep, pretend you're asleep. I felt like my insides were being ripped.

He started making those grunting noises again, like a pig. The pain was unbearable as he touched me for what seemed like for ever. He then got up, walked out, and I was left lying on the bed with my legs still wide open, shivering from the cold.

I reached for my quilt, which had been strewn across my radiator at the bottom of the bed. It felt warm, so I cuddled into it. I slipped my knickers and pyjamas back on. I didn't know what to do to ease the pain so I just lay there and cried.

I liked waking up in the morning because I could almost pretend what had happened in the night was a bad dream, but that morning I had a painful reminder – the worst I'd ever felt. I limped along the hall to the bathroom, wincing as I crouched on the toilet seat.

'Owww,' I yelped, as I went to the loo – it felt like I was peeing shattered glass. I crouched, paralysed by the pain, until it eased enough for me to walk again. I couldn't turn to anyone for help, I just had to swallow it and do my best to cope.

Starting a new school is the worst feeling in the world because you stick out like a sore thumb. It didn't help that my front teeth were so goofy they pushed my top lip out so I looked like Bugs Bunny. Everyone had formed their friendship groups by the final year of primary, so there was no way they would befriend an ugly duckling like me. I ate my packed lunch alone in the lunch hall, hoping someone nice would sit next to me. The more time I spent alone, the more time I had to think about the painful things that were happening.

I felt like I was a snail hiding in a transparent shell – I could see the world around me but I couldn't feel or touch or speak to anyone because I was keeping everything locked up inside. The playground at Ingrebourne Primary School in Harold Hill was huge and each year group had their own area, which they clung to. I spotted some girls from my class and edged up to them, hoping they would allow me into their circle. I braved a smile, doing my best not to expose my ugly mouth.

'You're the new girl?' one of the pretty girls asked.

'Yeah, that's right,' I said, trying to sound confident.

Some of the group started whispering and staring. They covered their mouths with their hands but it was obvious they were talking about me. I felt my cheeks burn with embarrassment as I tried to guess what mean things they were saying. I felt like a spare part, praying for the bell to ring so we would be called inside and I could hide behind my desk.

I now didn't have anyone to turn to. I had no one friendly at home and no friends at school. The only person who noticed me, brought me pain. I felt so confused.

So alone.

5

New Girl

'You're so fucking lazy!' Mum screamed, centimetres from my face. 'You never do fuck all to help me. All you're interested in is your fucking self.' I felt her angry spit spray my face.

'You lazy bitch,' she said, raising her hand. I stumbled back, getting ready to dodge her blow.

She glared at me with hatred.

'I HATE YOU!' I screamed, running for my bedroom. Nothing I did was good enough for my mum. I'd put the dinner on but she was furious it wasn't ready for when she got back from work. I'd been put in charge of making supper since Mum had taken up a job as secretary for a solicitor's office. I tried really hard to make yummy pasta dishes – I did my best to be a grown-up, but she always let me know when I'd failed. I felt like I'd turned into Cinderella since Mum had got a full-time job – I was banned from going out to the park unless I'd cooked and cleaned. Chores included hoovering, making the beds, doing the washing and keeping my mouth shut.

About this time, Dave also got a new job as a frozen-food

lorry driver because his old Rover had broken down. Mum had screamed at him to get a 'fucking job' because they had no 'fucking money' to pay for the car repairs. They were shouting so loudly downstairs the walls could have crumbled. When Dave asked me to come with him on his deliveries, I said yes because I was so desperate to get away from *her*. I didn't have any friends left to play with at the weekend. I'd become reliant on my stepdad – for treats, for making me feel wanted. I hated him touching me – I didn't like how he made me feel dirty – but he was the only person who made me feel special.

'This is my daughter,' he said to the manager of fast-food chain Wimpy as he pulled up with his burger delivery.

I reached out and shook the man's hand proudly. Dave called me his daughter – not his stepdaughter, his actual daughter. I beamed inside.

'If you're a good girl, I'll get you a burger,' Dave whispered to me.

'Amazing,' I said, grinning from ear to ear.

'Wait 'ere.' He winked.

I scrambled up into the lorry cabin and waited for Dave to get back. He came around the corner carrying a paper bag and a fizzy drink. His belly stuck out so much his buttons looked like they were going to pop off. He'd got a lot fatter in the five years I'd known him. And much balder – he now had a wisp of dark greasy hair which he combed over. He still had big sideburns growing down his face like ivy which looked silly. His neck was thick and his body was wide and stocky.

'It's your lucky day.' Dave grinned, handing me my treat.

I peered in the bag, and yelped with happiness to find some fries in there too. Dave looked pleased that he had won me over, again. He'd got himself a burger too and I watched as he shovelled it into his mouth, devouring it with barely a swallow between bites.

'You done?' he asked, his lips glistening with greasy burger fat. He wiped his mouth with his sleeve, rolled down the window and spat onto the tarmac.

'Right, on to our next delivery,' he said, turning the keys in the engine.

'Can I get another burger?' I asked.

'You don't want to be getting fat now, do ya, Flossy,' he smirked.

Any reference to my being fat made me recoil into my shell. I felt exposed and folded my arms protectively across my chest. We didn't usually talk about my body, and we never spoke about the things he liked to do to me in the night, during our time together in the day. We'd chat about normal things that I guess every father and daughter did. He'd speak to me in his harsh Northern Irish voice, peppering it with lots of effing and blinding. He liked to let rip at other drivers. 'You fuckin' cunt' was his favourite phrase. Sometimes we would drive for miles without saying a word, other times he'd speak about mundane things like his to-do list or something he'd seen on TV.

My stepdad was like Jekyll and Hyde – the Dave I got to see in the day and the monster in my room at night.

I went on a lot of lorry trips with Dave just after I started secondary school at Bedfords Park, Harold Hill, because we were sent home for a couple weeks due to an asbestos scare. I'd only been back a short time before Mum pulled Blake and me out because Blake was being bullied. I was sent to Frances Bardsley School for Girls.

Going to an all-girls school was bad enough, but starting six months after everyone else had joined was hell. I was back to being the new girl when everyone else had already formed their friendship groups. And to make things worse, I now had a brace like a train track running across my top and bottom teeth, which pushed my lips out even further, making me even more ugly, even more unlikeable.

Mum didn't take me on my first day, so I had to make my own way there on the bus. I sat on the back seat, nervously ironing out the pleats of my bottle-green uniform skirt with the flat of my hand. I hated wearing skirts because baring my legs made me feel exposed, just like when I wore my nightie in bed.

The bus driver dropped me off at the end of a long driveway lined with big trees. I could just make out the school buildings, but to a kid it appeared miles off. I pulled my rucksack onto both shoulders and started walking. My feet felt like lead as my nerves slowed me down. All I could think about was how I wished I was walking into class with a trendy satchel and not my cheap tatty rucksack. Maybe then the other girls would like me?

'There's no way I'm spending any fucking money on a fucking satchel when you can have a perfectly decent rucksack,' Mum shouted at me when I dared to ask her to buy me one for my new school.

I never asked for gifts from her. *Why couldn't she just do this one thing for me?* I really believed it would help me make friends. I clung to the shoulder straps as I walked along the corridor of giant trees. I felt tiny under their ginormous branches; it was like I was in some spooky horror film. My stomach was leaping somersaults by the time I reached the reception area, as the thought of sticking out as the new girl made me feel sick.

'Tina Moore?' confirmed the receptionist, peering over her glasses.

'Yes,' I mumbled reluctantly.

'You're late,' she scolded.

It was to be the first of a hundred tellings-off that I was to endure at Frances Bardsley. Thanks to my mum, I learnt that being told off was the only way to get attention.

'This is Tina, she'll be joining us from today,' my teacher introduced me to the class.

I kept my mouth clasped shut so as not to reveal my train tracks. Everyone's eyes were on me and I hated it. I walked straight past the empty desks at the front and tucked myself away at the back of the class. No one can stare at me here, I sighed with relief.

The bell for breaktime sounded and the room was filled with the deafening sound of textbooks slamming shut and chairs screeching backwards. I followed the crowd of girls as they pushed through the door and made their way outside to the playground. I didn't like lessons but I hated break more because I was on my own. I drifted off to a quiet corner and leant back against the fence, watching all the other girls play and have fun. It was January, and freezing, and all I had was a thin bottle-green V-neck jumper to keep me warm. I cuddled myself and hunched my shoulders forward to brace myself from the icy wind. I recognised a group from my class who were playing French skipping:

'England, Ireland, Scotland, Wales,' they sang in chorus, as one of the girls jumped over the rope tied between the legs of the other two. She screeched as she was caught out on the last hop.

'You're out, you're out.' The others giggled, as she threw up her arms with defeat. A small crowd had now formed to watch the entertainment.

'Donna's next,' one of the girls announced. Up stepped a very pretty girl with perfect features. She was tall and thin, with glossy chestnut hair that parted like curtains across her chiselled cheekbones. It didn't take a genius to work out she was the popular girl by the way the crowd parted for her like she was a celebrity. She threw her head back with laughter, revealing a perfect set of straight white teeth. She was everything I wanted to be: thin, pretty, popular and, above all, happy.

Her spell had worked on me, as I was drawn to the queen bee like all the others. I walked over to the crowd to watch Donna skip. The girls were squealing with excitement as she bounced perfectly over the ropes as if she was dancing.

'Whoooo,' everyone cheered, as Donna broke the record for the highest level. She threw her hands in the air as if she had won Olympic Gold.

'Who's next?' they chanted.

I don't know if I was driven by envy or anger, but something about watching Donna's performance had angered me and I wanted to prove that I was worth something too.

'I'll do it,' I said, stepping forward. The crowd parted for me but not quite in the same way – this time with disbelief. A cackle of laughter echoed across the playground.

'How are you going to get your fat legs between the ropes?' one of the girls sniggered.

I felt my cheeks burn red as everyone stared and laughed. The truth was I wasn't actually fat, I was just much taller and more developed, but girls are quick to pick up on insecurities and I would have smelt of self-loathing from what my stepdad was doing to me. I bowed my head and turned and walked away like a dog with its tail between its legs. I could still hear the cackles from afar as I slumped back against the fence. I looked at the ground to stop anyone seeing my tears, and watched as they splashed onto the concrete.

Dingalingaling. I was saved by the bell.

I waited for everyone to stream past so I could make my way back to class alone. I took a different route past the outdoor swimming pool, and coming from the other direction was Miss Popular herself: Donna. A fire of fury sparked alight inside my gut.

I hate you, I hate you. The red mist rose across my eyes. I couldn't stand the way she walked like she didn't have a care in the world. I'd never felt anger like it and I didn't know how to control it. The fire exploded through my arms and I turned to follow Donna and pushed her in the back. She lurched forward almost smacking into a wall. It felt amazing seeing her suffer – I wanted to go for her again. I wound my arm back ready for round two but Donna was quicker, and spun around to face her attacker. She narrowed her eyes like a cat, hissing at me with disgust.

She shrieked with anger as she flung her fist at my face.

I flew back with the force. My mouth burnt – the cow had caught my lip on my brace. I dabbed my face and my fingers turned crimson with blood. I looked up, hoping for sympathy, but Donna had already gone. I wasn't sure if I wanted to cry or scream, I felt so confused by what had happened; I didn't know where this angry Tina had come from but I liked her. My lip was throbbing but I blocked out the pain the same way I'd done so many times before.

I was late for class and the corridor was so quiet now it could have been a ghost school. The door of the girls' toilets creaked open, adding to the eeriness. The walls were plastered with graffiti and the sterile stench was like a hospital. I checked the mirror for the damage and it was much worse than I'd thought – my lip was sliced and blood was smeared across my cheek.

'You idiot, Tina,' I spat at my reflection. I could hear my mum's voice scolding me.

I ran the taps to scrub away the blood but this time I saw something different in the mirror. A smile crept across my face as I realised the potential to milk the situation for attention.

'You're late, Tina,' the teacher scolded.

'Sorry, miss,' I replied, shuffling through the door. I lifted my head and turned to face the class. I must have counted a dozen gasps as they saw the blood smeared across my face. I faked my best pained expression as I walked to my desk, but inside I was dancing. Donna flashed me a look of hate, which was the icing on the cake. Everyone kept turning around to stare at my injuries and I could hear them whispering about me. Everyone was talking about *me*. I spent the lesson watching the clock tick down to break time, so I could bask in my glory some more.

Dingalingalingggg, the bell drilled.

I stood up to leave, but I was stopped in my tracks.

'Are you OK?' gasped one of the girls.

'What happened to you?' another one chipped in. Within minutes a big group had gathered around me. I wanted to squeal, I was so happy, but I had to keep up the charade.

'Donna hit me,' I mumbled.

'Ugh,' everyone gasped.

'You need to see Nurse and get that cleaned up,' a girl with long blonde hair said.

'Or it could get infected and you might have to have your face amputated,' she exaggerated.

Everyone let out another gasp. I didn't go to see the nurse that afternoon because I didn't want anyone wiping away my war wounds. I kept the blood on my face until home time so I could get as much attention as possible. I didn't want to go home and be ignored again. I wanted this day to last for ever.

Mum was still at work when I got in so I got on with preparing the dinner. She came home in a mood, slamming the front door behind her.

'Where's my fucking fags?' she shouted, throwing an empty box of Superkings onto the floor. My whole body tensed as I waited for her attack on me.

'Oi, Flossy, when you've finished up in the kitchen, you can go to the shops for me,' she ordered. I nodded obediently. She handed me the cash, not even batting an eyelid at my cut lip, not even asking me how my first day at school was. I should have expected as much. Mum was slouched on the sofa flicking through the channels by the time I got back. I dished up, giving her the biggest portion of pasta.

'Blake, dinner's on the table!' I yelled up the stairs. I handed Mum her plate as she and Dave never sat with us at mealtimes.

'Thanks,' she muttered begrudgingly. 'What's happened to your face?' she then asked, finally noticing.

'I got into a fight,' I replied, bracing myself.

'You've only been at that school five fucking minutes and you're already getting yourself in trouble?' she yelled, her cheeks turning red with anger. 'You're a fucking nightmare,' she spat.

I edged backwards towards the stairs.

'Go to your fucking room,' she ordered. If she hadn't had a plate full of food, she would have hit me around the head.

I guess I should have been grateful that she noticed at all, I thought, slamming my fist against the wall. I pulled off my socks and dug my nails into my feet. Over the past few weeks I'd got into a habit of picking at my skin whenever I felt angry. I picked, and dug deeper, until the skin around my nails and sides of my feet bled and then I'd stop. Feeling pain before bed seemed to be the only way to send me to sleep now. It counteracted the pain and loneliness I was feeling inside.

I woke up the next morning with a spring in my step, as I hoped my cut lip would have bought me some friends, but I should have known better. Donna had spread the word that I had started the fight and now everyone was whispering about me, but for all the wrong reasons.

'Psycho,' one of the girls chanted as I walked over to my desk.

I took a deep breath and carried on. I wasn't feeling as strong today so I recoiled into my shell and hid from the world. I don't think I spoke to one person that day, and then I had to endure the bus ride home, being teased. I'd spent the day in hell only to return to another hell.

Dave was working again that night so I only had Mum to turn to for help with my English homework. I could understand everything perfectly, but no matter how hard I tried I couldn't spell. The letters would just get jumbled in my head.

'Mum, how do you spell "gardening"?' I asked.

'What?'

'How do you spell . . .' I started.

'Look it up in a bloody dictionary,' she snapped.

But to look up the word, I need to know how to spell it, I wanted to scream at her. I slammed my book shut and stomped up to bed.

'Don't even fucking think about going out to the park until you've finished it!' Mum screamed up the stairs. I thumped my feet so hard on the steps it made the staircase shudder.

'I hate you,' I barked, throwing my exercise book across my bedroom. I didn't know where all this anger was coming from but I felt like I wanted to punch someone, the wall, even myself. I lay on my bed for hours, dreaming up ways that I could make friends with the girls in my class. I drifted off, believing I finally had the answer.

I woke up to the sound of Dave steaming into Blake's room to give him another hiding. I'd also overslept, but Dave was treating me more like a princess than ever and would let me off with murder. I'd started to wonder if that was why Mum hated me so much. *Did she resent the fact that Dave gave me special treatment?* I pulled open my drawer and scooped out several handfuls of the gifts from my stepdad into my rucksack. I had so many hairsprays and mousses now, I could barely shut the drawer.

I could still hear Dave's fists pounding into Blake as I crept past and slipped out the front door. My bag was so heavy, I thought I was going to topple backwards. I leant forward, charging for the bus; I wasn't going to be late for class again, I wasn't going to stick out again.

Luckily the girls had got bored with calling me names but I had turned invisible instead. I tried smiling at some of the friendlier faces in my class as I walked to my desk but they stared through me. No one wanted to be seen to be my friend. *Come on, Tina, you can do this.* I gritted my teeth. I just needed a chance to show them I wasn't the freak I saw in the mirror. I spent the whole of lesson time going over my plans, obsessively thinking about what I was going to do and say. The teacher's voice sounded a million miles away.

The bell finally rang for break and everyone scrambled for the playground. I heaved my rucksack onto both shoulders and followed. Donna was standing in the centre of the playground with her usual group of admirers. I could hear my heart beat in my ears as I strode over to her, trying my best to hide my fear. She stopped in the middle of her sentence to stare at me, making everyone's heads turn. I heard a couple of gasps as I got close and threw the rucksack from my back.

'Does anyone want some hair products or make-up?' I asked. Inside I was trembling.

'What?' one of the girls asked like I was a freak.

I crouched down and unzipped my bag to reveal the mountain of Dave's presents.

'My stepdad buys me so many presents, I can't use them all,' I boasted, as if I had the best dad in the world.

The girls peered in, and one by one they started pulling out my gifts.

'Hair mousse,' one of them gasped. 'Wow, you're so lucky to have a dad like that,' she said enviously.

I grinned, as my plan had worked. The presents may have cost me, but at least they could buy me a friend for the day.

6

The Penny Drops

'HELP!' I screamed. 'Mum, help me ...'
Where are you? Why can't you hear me?

'MUUUUM, HELP ME!' I yelled so loud my throat grated. 'Somebody save me,' I whimpered, tears streaming down my face.

But no one could hear me.

I thrashed my arms from left to right, trying to escape, but I was trapped.

'Nooooo!' I yelled and jolted myself awake.

'Where am I?' I gasped, heaving for air; my chest was so tight I thought I was going to explode. I was dripping in sweat and my sheets were icy cold with damp. My dream had been so real I thought I was still in it. It was the fourth night in a row I'd dreamt of being buried alive in a glass coffin with just a tiny tube feeding me air. No matter how hard I screamed, no one could hear, and I'd always wake up at the point when I was about to pass out.

Something had changed over the past nine months. I was getting terrible nightmares that would often leave me in tears. I'd never had a temper before but now I often wanted to punch something or someone. The pain in my private parts had also got much worse, so that some days I could barely sit at my desk. I'd started to forget what it felt like to not be in agony.

I couldn't tell anyone, as talking about your 'bits' when you are eleven years old was too embarrassing for words. I didn't know if anyone else had started their periods; it wasn't the sort of thing we would talk about in the playground. And although I hated what my stepdad did, I still didn't know it was wrong. As far as I was concerned, that's what all dads did with their daughters.

That was until the lesson that changed everything.

If I thought talking about my period was bad enough, imagine a class full of eleven- and twelve-year-old girls talking about sex for the first time in their lives. I'd watched the girls laugh and joke all morning about what our sex education lesson would be like. I had no idea how babies were made; they could have been flown in by storks for all I knew.

The class was on the first floor, because I remember staring out of the window and seeing the treetops. Our teacher seemed more embarrassed than us, as she flushed scarlet when she handed out small square pouches with something circular inside.

'These are condoms,' she stammered. 'They are used as contraception to stop women getting pregnant,' she continued, pinning her hair nervously behind her ears.

'Where do you put it, miss?' one of the naughty girls asked, making the class snigger.

'Well, it goes on the man's penis . . .' she started.

'Ewwww, it's all slimy!' someone shouted.

'Look out,' one of the girls said, as she flicked it across the room like an elastic band.

'Girls, behave,' the teacher snapped, and we broke down into fits of giggles. The whole thing was embarrassingly funny.

The teacher crossed the room and wheeled out the TV and VCR machine. She was wearing a big-knit cardigan over a white shirt tucked into a knee-length skirt, and flat shoes, and her face looked like she wished she was anywhere but with us. She fiddled with the VCR, muttering under her breath as she re-checked the connection to the television.

'Ahem,' she cleared her throat. We were still all too busy sniggering.

'OK, class!' she shouted. 'I'm going to show you a video, so pay attention,' she said. She dimmed the lights and took a seat at the side of the room. The narrator had a voice like he was presenting a nature documentary.

'When a man and a woman are in a relationship, they make a baby together,' the narrator explained, and across the screen flashed a drawing of a man entering a woman.

'So is that how babies are made?' someone asked.

'Yes, shhhh, listen!' she snapped.

But I'd listened enough. I felt the colour drain from my face as I realised what my stepfather had been doing to me. The room started to spin and I wanted to be sick. The video was an electric shock, unearthing the memories I'd buried for the past year …

. . . I was transported to my bedroom where I was woken by the touch of Dave's coarse fingers on my back as he slid them over my bum, tugging me onto my side. He pulled my pyjamas off just like all those other times before.

'You're so lovely,' he drooled over me. I could hear he was on his knees by my bedside. I heard his body twist as he fiddled with something on the floor. *What is it? Is it that horrible sticky cream again?* I waited to hear the lid unscrew, but nothing. He turned back to me and I could feel his hot breath across my stomach as he examined me closely. He waited and waited and then I flinched as I felt something cold between my legs.

'Relax,' Dave whispered.

My heartbeat turned wild with fear. *Ba-boom. Ba-boom.*

He rubbed the cold thick object across me, back and forth.

Ba-boom ba-boom. My heart was racing.

He pressed a button and it started vibrating. It was shaking and humming and I hated it. I wanted him to stop. I wanted to look at what he was doing to me but I was too scared to open my eyes and show him I was awake. Being asleep was the only protection I had left.

'Do you like that?' he whispered, edging the cold vibrating object between my legs.

'You like that, don't you?' he went on, as he pushed the object inside me.

A bullet of pain shot inside me, and I felt like I was being ripped in half. He moved it in and out, in and out. I imagined myself standing in the park – the grass was bright green and it was sunny. I kept imagining until the pain got so bad I went numb.

I don't know how long he used it for, but it felt like for ever. Dave then got off his knees and leant over me. I felt his moist breath, down there; he was breathing so heavily I got wafts of his disgusting cigarette breath. He stuck out his slimy tongue and tried to lick me.

'Tsk,' he snapped, irritated he couldn't reach me properly from the side . . .

The teacher must have said something funny as my flash-back was invaded by the roar of the class erupting in laughter . . . It wasn't enough to jolt me back into the class-room though, as their giggles fizzled out again, and all I could hear was Dave's heavy breathing, panting over me.

I heard him get off his knees again and noises that sounded like he was taking off his pants. *Please don't make me clasp my hand around 'it'.*

Ba-boom. Ba-boom. My heart was pumping so fast I thought I was going to explode.

My body stiffened as I heard another noise. *What is it?* I strained my ears, it sounded like a wrapper being torn open. Dave hovered by my bed for a moment while he rolled something onto himself. The numb feeling inside had worn off and the pain had set in. He then did something he'd never done before – he climbed onto my bed. He grabbed my tiny ankles with his sweaty palms and pushed my legs up. I let them flop back down – I was asleep. He lifted them again, more roughly this time, but I let them fall back onto my mattress.

'Come on, you'll like it, help me!' he snapped with irritation.

Help you? I want you to disappear, I wanted to scream. I had a terrible feeling things were about to get much worse. He clambered on top of me, squashing me with his fat body. I could feel his big belly smothering mine; his stinking breath was on my face. I couldn't bear it.

I wouldn't open my legs for him, so he pushed his hard penis against me like he was chiselling me open. He thrust, and pushed harder, and I felt a sharp pain as he rammed inside me. The stinging got worse as he gathered steam and moved faster and harder on top of me. My tiny body jerked up and down the mattress like I was rag doll. His breathing got heavier, he pushed deeper and then let out a giant grunt of satisfaction. He panted over my face and then peeled himself off, leaving a sticky trail of sweat across my body . . .

I squirmed around in my classroom chair as I relived the pain.

. . . I kept my eyes clasped shut as I heard my stepdad leave and then I opened them a tiny bit; I needed to know he wasn't still in my room. He was just wearing his pants when he crept back into my mum's bed.

I lay glued to the bed, unable to move for the throbbing pain. It felt like I'd had a knife jabbed inside me and slashed around. I was terrified because I had no idea what he had done to me. I hobbled to the bathroom, scared of what I might find . . .

I squirmed again in my chair as I remembered the pain of going to the loo.

It burnt like pouring hot lemon juice in a cut. I remembered dabbing myself with the toilet tissue and seeing blood. The bathroom started to spin as I watched the blobs spread like ink on blotting paper . . .

The bell for break went, shaking me from my flashback. I was gasping for breath just like when I'd woken from one of my nightmares.

I can't tell you how many times my stepfather had raped me by the time I was eleven because I'd blocked the horrific memories until that moment. The penny had dropped that day, as I learnt that what Dave was doing to me wasn't what all fathers did with their daughters; it was what couples do to make babies.

The girls were like a herd of elephants as they crashed past my desk for the door, but I couldn't hear a thing. I sat there all on my own like a rabbit stuck in the headlights. My world as I knew it had fallen away from under my feet, as I realised what my stepdad was doing to me was very very wrong.

I don't remember much about the rest of the day, only the bus ride home as it seemed to go on for ever. Thankfully no one was home when I got back so I dived into the cupboard and scooped up a handful of chocolate bars – Bounty, Twix and Mum's favourite: Fry's Chocolate Cream. I ran up to my room and turned on the Bangles' 'Eternal Flame' as loud as I could to drown out the horrific images in my mind.

I sang along, tears streaming down my face.

As soon as the song finished, I played it back again, and

again. I unwrapped the chocolate bars and pushed them into my mouth one after the other. I hated myself and I wanted to get fat so *he* would hate me too, so he wouldn't come near me again.

7

Road to Hell

Once you open a leaky tap it's impossible to stop it dripping.

Our sex education class had opened a Pandora's box of memories. I couldn't stop the flashbacks and I wasn't strong enough to block the fresh ones any more.

My stepdad was having sex with me once, sometimes twice, a week, and I didn't know how to stop him. I couldn't tell my mum because we didn't talk, we screamed at one another. I hadn't made any friends at school to confide in and, even if I did, I would be too ashamed to tell them about my dirty secret.

It all made sense why I'd felt so angry over the past months – I'd been bottling up the truth. Now I realised my dad was preying on me, I felt angrier than ever before. I was desperate for someone to save me, so I did everything I could to get attention. I turned myself into the class clown, provoking the teachers just like I would do my mum. If the teacher asked me a question, I'd come back with some sarcastic reply.

'Tina, what's the capital of England?' the teacher asked.

'Romford, of course, miss,' I grinned.

The class erupted in laughter while I enjoyed keeping a straight face.

'Very clever, Tina. You're not doing yourself any favours,' she said, sighing with irritation as she walked back to the blackboard.

How dare she turn her back on me. I could feel my venom bubbling.

'But you called me clever, miss,' I provoked.

'Enough, Tina!' she snapped.

But I hadn't had enough. I wanted her to turn around and look at me.

'But, miss . . .' I started. But before I could finish, she had hurled a piece of chalk at my head.

'Owwww!' I shrieked, and the class fell silent. It hurt like hell but I was just happy to be the centre of attention. The new Tina quickly earned me friends; a couple of the rebellious girls in my year asked me to join them for a smoke around the back of the school fence. I was terrified they would see through my act, so I stepped up the bravado, desperate to cling on to them.

'Have you smoked before?' Sarah asked, leaning her tall lanky body back against the fence.

'Yeah, course I have,' I lied. I hated the smell of smoke because it reminded me of 'him'.

'Have a puff of this then,' Sarah said, handing me her cigarette. It felt like a test, as both girls stared at me closely. *Come on, Tina, don't mess this up*, the scolding voice in my head screamed at me again. I leant back with my foot on the fence, faking my best tough-girl look, and took a long inhale on the cigarette.

'*Euuuhahahaa*,' I spluttered. My cheeks blushed crimson, as the girls gave each other a look as if to say I was a fraud.

'What are you smoking?' I asked, screwing up my face, trying to blame it on the brand of cigarettes. I was determined to fit in, so I took another puff, fighting through the burn in my throat.

'We like hiding back here,' said the other girl, Kelli, who had dark hair and a round face. 'Gets us away from those stupid teachers telling us what to do all the time,' she grumbled.

'Yeah, I hate being told what to do,' I joined in, kicking a stone across the grass to show I was tough. I just wanted to be liked, to belong.

By the end of the first year at secondary school, I'd got myself a reputation for being a naughty kid with a nasty temper. The girls had nicknamed me the 'Tinanator', after Arnold Schwarzenegger in the film *Terminator*, because I lashed out when anyone upset me. I couldn't fight back in my bedroom so I brought out the anger in the classroom.

It had been raining so hard one morning that we were allowed to spend our lunch break inside the classroom. Everyone splintered off into their small groups, just like in the playground, only it was much easier to overhear the whispers. I was now bingeing on chip sandwiches every day and had laid out my lunch and a pudding of chocolate bars across on the desk. One of Donna's friends deliberately barged into me, knocking me from my perch and sending my chip butty flying across the room.

'I just saved you from getting even fatter,' she taunted, strutting across the room like a peacock.

I looked at the chips strewn across the floor, and then at her. A red mist rose in my eyes and I charged across the room like a bull after a matador. Everything around me blurred into slow motion as my vision tunnelled on her. I thrust out my fist to smack her face, but tripped on the table leg. The force of my punch was so hard, so angry, I came crashing down with the weight of an elephant. The room went dark and then faded to black as I passed out.

'Tina, wake up!' someone shouted in my ear.

'Wake up,' they said again. The voice sounded miles away, like I was looking at myself from high above.

'WAKE UP!'

My eyes finally opened. I'd knocked myself out for twenty seconds but it seemed like an hour had past. I looked up at half-a-dozen eyes staring back at me.

'Are you OK?' one of my classmates asked. They didn't know how high my pain threshold was. The bump on my head was just a scratch compared with what my stepdad was doing to my insides.

'Yeah, I'm fine.' I shrugged, brushing the dust off my shirt. I felt so calm since the knock it was hard to know where the anger had come from. It was like I had a monster inside me that took over my body when I needed protection. And the worse Dave's touching got, the more the monster would rear its ugly head.

Tough Tina was my shield but it wasn't the real me. The real Tina was incredibly lonely, a little girl who spent almost every night crying, who more than anything, wanted a normal childhood. I was robbed of the simplest things that all the other girls took for granted. I couldn't play at friends' houses after school because I had chores to do for my mum. I couldn't invite friends to my mine because I was ashamed and afraid of my family.

But I longed to do the things kids my age did, just once. So one afternoon I asked Liz and Mel to catch the bus home with me, knowing that Dave and Mum wouldn't be back until later that evening. I should have known better than to break out of my prison.

I had just turned twelve and loved playing lady of the house, fetching the girls orange squash and offering them a choice from Mum's massive chocolate-bar collection. I wanted them to think I was a friend worth having because I had lots to offer.

'You can have anything you like from there,' I boasted, as I pulled open my secret drawer full of Dave's presents.

'Wow, Tina, how lucky are you?' Mel gawped.

'That eye shadow would look really nice on you,' I said, handing it to her. I smiled as she opened it up and dabbed it across her eyelid. I hated myself so much I believed the only thing I had going for me was the presents I could give away. *I'm ugly. Why else would they want to waste their time with me unless I can offer them something?*

'I've got a few games we could play,' I suggested. I didn't want them to leave.

'What you got?' Mel asked, rummaging through my goody drawer.

'Blockbuster?' I said, pulling out the box from the shelf.

'I love Blockbuster,' Liz squealed, brushing her black curls out of her eyes.

I set up the game in the living room and let them get started while I put on the dinner. The fear of what Mum would do to me if it wasn't on the table pulled me back into the kitchen.

'Do you want more squash?' I yelled through to them, as I quickly threw some potatoes and vegetables in pots to boil. 'Why can't I just have one night off?' I muttered under my breath.

'Tina, it's your go!' Mel shouted. I joined them in the living room and sat cross-legged on the floor. I couldn't remember the last time I played a game in my house; it felt really strange doing something fun, as if it was wrong to be enjoying myself.

'Damn you,' Mel shrieked, as I was the first to get five questions correct in a row.

'Ha, you lose,' I cheered, relaxing into it. For an hour I got to be a child again and the weight I carried on my shoulders lifted. I didn't think about Dave touching me, about my mum hating me, about fighting with Blake – I was having fun with my friends. I was just celebrating my fourth win in a row when I was brought down to earth, with a crash.

'Is something burning?' Mel sniffed.

'The dinner!' I shrieked, scrambling to my feet and running into the kitchen to find smoke billowing. Panic bolted through me as I examined the damage – I'd burnt the bottoms of Mum's brand-new pots.

'Noooo!' I screamed, scrubbing the pans vigorously in soapy water.

'Just tell your mum it was an accident,' Mel said, trying to calm me down.

'You don't understand, she's going to go mad,' I snapped. If it wasn't anger raging through me it was fear. I seemed to spend my life flitting between the two and I was exhausted. I told the girls to leave before Mum got back. They nervously said goodbye and left me at the sink.

'Please come off,' I pleaded, using my nails to try to scrape off the marks. 'Please,' I whimpered. 'I promise I'll never have anyone over to stay again.' I scrubbed until I couldn't feel my arms any longer, but the shape of the potatoes was still embedded.

'It's not fair!' I shouted, throwing the sponge across the kitchen. I slid down the cupboards, landing in a pathetic heap on the floor. I tucked my knees tightly into my chest and rocked back and forth as the tears fell onto my school uniform, gluing my straggly hair to my cheeks.

It was pointless letting my mum find me in this mess because she wouldn't feel sorry for me. It was better to stand up and be ready to dodge the blows. I heard the key in the lock and I threw on my armour.

'What the bloody hell is that smell?' She coughed, stepping into the hallway.

'Tina?' she yelled, immediately blaming me.

She walked into the kitchen to find me standing with my

back to the sink, my arms clasped nervously behind me. Mum narrowed her eyes and looked me up and down.

'I've had a bit of an accident,' I said, looking down at the ground.

'What do you mean, a fucking accident?' she barked.

'I overcooked the vegetables and now I can't get the marks out,' I mumbled.

She pushed me out of the way and reached into the sink. I could hear the growl in her throat as she examined the mess. Mum spun around and slapped me across the face.

'You stupid bitch,' she spat.

I clasped my burning cheek in my hand trying to fight the tears.

'You fucking idiot, you can't do anything fucking right!' she yelled. Her eyes were wild like a crazed animal. I edged backwards as I saw her raise her arm again, and I turned and ran for my room.

'Little fucking bitch!' she screamed up the stairs.

I threw myself onto my bed and buried my head into my pillow, punching my hands into my mattress. I didn't mean to burn the pots. I just wanted to have fun with my friends. I pulled open my drawer and scooped out a handful of chocolate that I'd been hoarding. I lay on my side and pushed it into my mouth, one after the other. The sugar hit was comforting and I knew it was the only supper I'd be getting that night.

When Dave told me he was taking me on one of his overnight lorry drives at the weekend, I didn't fight it – a burger and chips was better than another smack in the face from Mum. I'd lost all sense of who was causing me the most pain. When Mum was cruel I turned to Dave because he was the only person who made me feel wanted. I'd become dependent on him for treats and attention and what I'd come to believe love was. I plodded down the stairs with my sleeping bag and pyjamas tucked under my arm, accepting what was in store. Dave had never touched me anywhere except my bedroom, so all I could do was pray the ritual wouldn't change.

Mum was on the sofa, slurping a cup of tea, her body slouched over like an old pillow. She barely lifted her eyes to wave us off.

'See you when you get back,' she said, her eyes glued to the box.

I still hated her for smacking me for burning the pots, but I wanted her to save me. I wanted my mum to look up and ask her husband why he was taking me, and not Blake or Jonathan, on an overnight lorry trip.

Look at me! I screamed at her through my eyes, hugging the sleeping bag into my chest.

'Have fun,' she said dismissively. The candle flicker of hope blew out.

I clambered up into the lorry cab and threw my sleeping bag onto the tiny bed behind the seats. The cabin smelt of sickly sweet vanilla wafting from the air freshener dangling on the rear-view mirror. The side pockets were stuffed full of empty cigar packets and junk-food wrappings, and the ashtray was full to the brim with fag stubs. We were driving from one end of the country to the other to make a delivery.

Dave told me some of his new routes would mean two nights on the road. I asked him if he found it lonely.

'It's better than listening to yer mum rabbiting on,' he said, mimicking her big mouth with his hand.

He seemed as fed up with her screaming as I was. I often wondered why he put up with the way she shouted at him. *Why doesn't he just leave like my real dad did?* As a kid I didn't really twig the significance of me as the incentive for him to stick around. We were on the road for hours but somehow the time just flew. He'd listen to the radio and I'd doze off in the passenger seat. I looked forward to our pit stops at the services because he'd buy me ice cream and fizzy drinks.

The night drew in and I clambered over the back seat to change into my pyjamas. I lay down on the tiny bed as I wriggled my way into them, so Dave wouldn't be able to see me change in the rear-view mirror.

'You can sleep there and I'll sleep in the driver's seat,' Dave told me. I snuggled into my sleeping bag, pulling it tightly around me like a protective cocoon. The cabin was lit by the motorway lights but the motion of the lorry soon sent me to sleep. When I woke, we were parked in a lorry depot at a service station somewhere.

It was the sound of Dave trying to clamber over the seats that jolted me awake.

He huffed and puffed as he heaved his fat body over the central barrier, eclipsing the street light.

He reached out for my sleeping bag but couldn't quite grab it, so he lurched forward aggressively, tugging it down my legs. I squeezed my eyes shut; I couldn't bear to watch him attack me. He fished around again from above, swooping back and forth until he had hold of my pyjama bottoms, and then yanked them hard down to my knees. I held my breath as I waited for his next swoop.

'*Eughahaha*,' he coughed, spluttering his phlegm over my face.

I wanted to wipe it away but I was pretending to be asleep, so I had to let it drip as I pinned myself to the tiny mattress. He shoved his fingers hard into me. He could barely reach, so he thrust them in and out vigorously as he leant over the seat.

I heard the sound of a buckle jingling undone and his trousers coming off. Next, the familiar noise of a packet being torn open, which meant the worst bit was seconds away. He clambered over the seat and landed on top of me with his full weight. There was barely room for one person in the back let alone me and a fat lump like him. I could feel his erect penis pressing against my leg and his frustration at not being able to reach me properly. He pushed my limp body up against the back of the seat and tried to enter me that way.

'*Eugh*,' he growled with frustration. He rammed himself against me and entered me a bit. He tried to gather speed pressing me hard into the back of the seat. My neck was twisted so far into the corner, I felt like it was going to rip off my shoulders as he pounded me. I kept my eyes glued shut – I could never look at him because it would make the nightmare real, even though I was desperate to cry out with pain.

He eventually pulled out because he must have realised he'd break my neck if he kept going. He tugged at something on his penis and then he started making those groaning noises as he moved his hand backwards and forwards while I slid down the bed. My top was pushed up and my pants and pyjamas were wrapped around my ankles. I felt so dirty and ashamed and helpless. He kept going, panting more heavily as he played with himself. He let out a huge grunt as something thick and warm splattered between my legs. I felt it trickle – *Make it stop*. He reached into the front to grab a cloth and then wiped me down roughly. Then he climbed back into the front and I immediately put my knickers and bottoms on and wriggled into my sleeping bag. The pain in my neck was worse than my insides this time. I clutched it with both hands, hoping for a miracle to send me to sleep.

I drifted in and out of sleep, waking up to the shooting pain in my neck every time I stirred. The cab windows were steamed up from Dave's heavy breathing, which made the moon look like it was hidden by a thick layer of fog. I drifted off again . . . to be woken by the engine revving.

'I got you some breakfast,' Dave said, handing me a McDonald's McMuffin, like nothing had happened. The ache in my neck reminded me of the horror of the night, but Dave didn't say a word when he saw me rubbing it.

'Thanks,' I said. It was my reward for not screaming out last night.

We'd immediately slipped back into our father-and-daughter relationship, where nothing of the night before gets mentioned. I liked the way he swept it under the carpet because just the thought of discussing the intimate things he enjoyed doing to me made me feel terrible. I thought keeping it a secret was the only way to survive it. If only I had been grown up enough to understand that by keeping quiet I was prolonging my torture.

Dave twizzled the radio tuner until he found a song he liked. He nestled back into the driver's seat and started tapping the steering wheel along to his favourite singer – Enya. A smile crept across his face because Mum hated Enya and Dave only got to listen to her when Mum had gone to bed. I clutched my neck, as he drove along without a care in the world.

I'd been sitting for twenty-four hours but I was still exhausted by the time we got home. Every part of my body was now aching and all I wanted to do was climb into my bed and wake up the next day in a little less pain. Mum was still in the same place I had left her and she didn't even ask how my trip was. I limped up the stairs and heard her bark:

'You better fucking tidy away that sleeping bag.'

Her words bounced off my armour. I didn't have the strength to shout back at her. I sighed with relief as I closed my door and shut out the rest of the world. I shuffled around on my bed, trying to make myself comfortable but nothing was working and I could feel the anger bubbling. I threw back my quilt and kicked it to the bottom of my bed. I punched the wall but it didn't have the same release as before. The monster inside me wanted to get out and I could feel it tearing at my skin. I pushed myself forward to the edge of the bed and let out a howl of anger, slamming my fists down onto my thighs. I buckled forward in agony – the pain made my eyes stream – but the release was an incredible feeling. I needed to do it again, on my bare skin. I tugged my jeans down to my knees and raised my arms high:

WHACK – it sounded just like when Dave smacked Blake.

WHACK – my skin burnt.

WHACK – the anger and pain locked inside was seeping out of me.

My skin was stinging red but I could breathe again. I put on my PJs to hide the developing bruises and climbed back under my quilt. Before long I had drifted off into a deep sleep.

8

Writing on the Wall

I hobbled through the front door of our new house in Rush Green, flinching with every footstep. We'd only been in our new three-bedroom house in Meadow Road a week but Mum had already made herself at home on her beloved sofa.

'Ouch,' I shrieked as I tried to climb the stairs.

Mum looked over and pulled a face, as if to say, 'What have you done now?'

'*Oowwww*,' I howled, provoking her more.

'What the hell are you whining about?' she huffed.

'I think I sprained my ankle getting off the bus,' I whimpered.

'Come 'ere,' she barked.

I limped through the living room, wincing with every step. She rolled up my jeans to have a closer look.

'*Owwwww*,' I screamed.

'For fuck's sake, Flossy, this is all I need. Dave's not back so I'm gonna have to take you down the hospital,' she groaned. 'Where's my fucking fags? I'm going to need them,' she said, reaching down the sides of the sofa for the packet.

'Sorry, Mum, I really didn't mean to do it,' I pleaded, doing my best to balance on one leg.

'You will be sorry if you don't get in that car now; now get a move on,' she said, ushering me out the door. We sat in silence as she drove us to Oldchurch Hospital A&E, but inside I was smiling. Tonight, I wouldn't have to cook dinner. I had Mum's undivided attention.

We must have spent at least two hours waiting in the tropically hot, smelly A&E. Mum wouldn't stop moaning about the time she was wasting and the noisy people sitting next to us, but I didn't care – I was so glad to have her to myself. She could have been screaming at me and I still would have been happy.

'Tina,' the doctor called. I looked at Mum to ask her to come with me and she sighed deeply as she heaved herself up. We were led into a cubicle surrounded by a blue shower curtain just like the one I sat in six years earlier when Mum whipped me around the back of my head with my coat.

'So tell me where the pain is?' the doctor asked in a soothing voice.

'Ummm, my ankle hurts,' I mumbled, unable to look him in the eye. I felt myself go red; I never thought my lie would get this far. I'd discovered that if I angle my foot in such a way I could make it look swollen and I wanted to see if it would get my mum's attention. I was so happy to have her by my side I hadn't thought what would happen if a real doctor examined it.

'*Owwww,*' I lied when he squeezed it. He frowned, puzzled, and went in for a second feel.

'Ouch,' I snapped, pulling my leg back.

I made such a fuss about the pain that the doctor diagnosed me as having a possible sprain and sent me home on crutches. Mum let me sit on the sofa and arranged a stool with a pillow to put my leg up. I was in heaven.

'Mum, can I have some squash?' I asked, with my best puppy-dog eyes.

'Go get it yourself,' Blake spat, seething with jealousy from all the attention I was getting.

'How can I?' I said sarcastically, pointing to my ankle.

'Leave your sister alone,' Mum shouted at Blake as she fetched me a glass. This was better than I ever could have wished for. *Maybe Mum did love me after all?* That's all I wanted to know – that somewhere in her heart she was glad I was her daughter. That she missed me when Dave stole me away on his lorry trips. That, in fact, she didn't want Dave to take me away at all.

I still held a candle of hope that my mother would be the one to save me.

Attention is like a drug: the more you get the more you crave; and I had become an addict. Now I'd finally got my mum to notice me, I pushed her for more.

'Mum,' I called from my bedroom.

Nothing.

'*Muuuuum,*' I screeched.

Nothing. I got out of bed and shouted from the door.

'Mum, can I have some juice?' I yelled.

'No, you're in bed now, go to sleep,' she finally responded.

I'd only been on crutches for a couple of days but she'd

already lost interest in me. I didn't want to let her go, and seeing her slip away made me feel desperate.

WHACK – I thumped my fists onto my legs. WHACK, WHACK, WHACK. I couldn't control the anxiety churning my stomach, and hitting myself was a distraction. My legs were still blue and purple from the last time I'd beaten myself, but the bruises had become a comfort. I pulled my pillow from the headboard and drilled into it with my fists until I ran out of steam.

My fake sprain may have worn off on Mum but unexpectedly it kept my stepdad out of my room for the rest of the week. I hadn't even considered that it would have put him off touching me because he seemed oblivious to the pain he usually caused me. *I wonder what other things I can do to keep him out?* Wearing pyjamas had slowed him down, but it was no deterrent. Pretending to be asleep hadn't worked at all.

I've got it. A smile crept across my face. I'd spent the whole day plotting ideas. *I've got the answer, I've got the answer.*

My new bedroom in Rush Green was bigger than my last, and the view from my window was of lush green playing fields. I was woken on Saturday mornings by cheering fans, and I'd peep out to see huge stocky rugby players from Barking and Dagenham Club running up and down the pitch. My carpet was pink to match the curtains and I had a girly-white-and-flower valance sheet wrapped around my single bed. It was the kind of room I would have loved before I was ten, before he raped me. But I didn't feel like a girl any more.

My room was opposite the bathroom and next to Blake and Jonathan's, which in turn was next to Dave and Mum's room. My bedroom was the furthest from Mum's, so 'noise' was less likely to travel. Unlike the last place, I had no high hopes for this house. I didn't taunt myself any more with the hope that a new home would be a new start.

I was woken in the dead of night by the sound of the door creaking open. I hadn't got used to all the noises and smells that come with a new house. My room was at the back, but for some reason it was still lit up at night – bright enough to see my stepdad creep across my floor in just his pants. I shut my eyes and waited for the ritual touching to begin. He'd been drinking lots – I could smell it on his breath and seeping through his skin. Dave and Mum had been laughing and knocking back the booze and listening to music with Tony and Sue, a couple they had met from across the road. Mum must have gone to bed, and Dave thought he'd stop off at my room on his way there.

He knelt by my side and threw back the quilt to expose my body. I didn't have time to roll over, so he had a head start on pulling me into him. He wriggled my pyjama bottoms off, breathing heavily with brandy breath. I lay there, rigid as a board, for the first time unsure of what would happen next.

'Tsk,' he tutted with irritation, as he felt my knickers. He then got off his knees and walked out, wasting no more time on me. I could breathe again. I waited for him to settle into his marital bed before I crept to the bathroom. I propped my leg up on the toilet seat.

'Ouch.' I flinched as I struggled to pull out a dry tampon from inside me. It was stuck. I tugged harder, slowly easing it out. I pulled my knickers back up but made sure the sanitary towel I'd stuck inside them stayed until the morning, just in case Dave changed his mind about leaving me alone.

Pretending I was still having my period was the only deterrent I could think of, as Dave always left me alone whilst I was bleeding. He'd felt the pad in my pants and backed off. *How long could I make my period last?* I prayed I had enough sanitary towels to play it out for a week longer. Mum always made Dave buy the extra big pads. I hated sleeping with them in my knickers because they were big and sweaty, but they were a million times better than the alternative.

For two weeks I was left in peace. He'd come into my room, check, then leave in a mood because he couldn't get what he wanted. Dave found another use for me in the end though. He rolled my body onto my side so I was facing him and let his pants drop to the ground. I could smell his groin in my face; I wanted to gag, but I kept my eyes pinned shut. His hand lunged forward and he grabbed my chin, clasping it in his sweaty hand. He squeezed my cheeks together like a vice, forcing my mouth open. I wanted to squeal but nothing came out. I'd lost my voice years ago. He edged his way forward and thrust his penis so deeply into my mouth I couldn't breathe. The salty taste, the smell, no air: I wanted to be sick. He thrust even deeper and I retched as it hit the back of my throat. I pulled back and tossed my head as far from him as I could, burying it into my big teddy bear. I could feel his eyes boring into my back as he hovered by my bed. *Would he try again? Please, no.*

He hovered there for a minute, sighing with frustration as I huddled into the fur of my teddy, as if it was going to save me. He turned and left and I peeped to check if he had really gone before I clambered out of my bed and dashed to the toilet. This time I scrubbed the evidence from my mouth. Thinking about what he had just done made me retch again. I smeared a massive dollop of toothpaste on my brush and scrubbed my teeth and my tongue and my gums so hard I was spitting blood. As the water washed the blood down the drain I wondered how my mum managed to sleep through all the noise. *Could she hear me in the bathroom now?* But I washed my thoughts away with the blood so I could stand a chance of getting back to sleep. Life had become about surviving.

My period was now a blessing in disguise but I dared not play it for longer than two weeks otherwise Dave might get wise to it. Taking off my armour was a scary feeling – the sanitary towels allowed my body to heal from being raped twice a week. I was just starting to remember what it felt like not to walk in pain, and I didn't want to go back there. I didn't have a choice though. My stepfather made up for lost time, and pounded me into the pink headboard on his next visit.

I'd got used to the burning sensation when I went to the loo but something felt very wrong 'down there' when we left for a family holiday to visit Dave's brother John in Ireland. As we drove on to the ferry in our gold Citroën, the parts that my stepdad liked to touch felt so itchy I wanted to scratch them with my nails. That panicky feeling of not knowing what was happening to my body revved up again, and the only way I could think of calming down was to run away. I left Mum, Dave and Jonathan queuing for soggy scrambled eggs and bacon at the canteen – luckily Blake had stayed with Nan (Mum's mum) so that was one less fight to worry about – while I slipped away to the front of the ferry.

The sea was a glacial blue, just like my mum's eyes, and the sky looked angry, as if it was going to explode. I yearned to be on the other side of the glass so the icy gale could calm the itching down. 'No going on deck, Flossy,' Mum had warned. I imagined myself there instead – the wind bashing me from side to side.

Is that why I never tell Dave to leave me alone? Because I'm scared he'll explode and beat me just like he punches Blake?

The rain sounded like a nail gun as it fired against the ferry windows.

Why can't I be stronger and tell him to get off me? Tell him no? It's all my fault for letting it happen to me.

'YOU'RE SO WEAK!' I screamed at the sea. My words were lost into the noise of the storm.

I scratched away my tears with my sleeve and found an empty row of seats where I could be alone, until Mum yelled for me to get back in the 'fucking car' because we were 'fucking leaving'. The rain was lashing as we drove on shore, turning everything into a grey blur, and I thought, *Some holiday this is going to be*. I rubbed a hole in the window condensation with my sleeve and jolted back in horror. The streets were lined with men dressed head to foot in black, carrying guns. *Real guns.* I froze as an armoured car pulled out in front of us, followed by several British Army soldiers, their boots sounding like thunder as they ran along the concrete. I had no idea what was going on. I was just a kid, and terrified we were going to be shot.

'What's happening?' I panicked, my head darting left to right. Mum and Dave were too busy bickering over directions to the caravan park to calm me down. I shrank into my seat and wanted to hide from this dangerous place.

'We'll be OK as long as we don't get lost,' I overheard Dave say, as he drove past dingy houses with boarded-up windows. There was graffiti everywhere; some of the buildings were burnt to the ground; others had barbed wire around them. I saw bullet holes in the walls and I panicked.

'How will we know if we get lost?' I badgered.

'If we see paintings on the wall, then we are in trouble,' he grumbled.

'Why?' I asked, desperate for an explanation.

'Oh, for God's sake, don't they teach you anything at school?' Mum snapped.

I had no idea that we were in the middle of a war between the Catholics and the Protestants. All I could see were guns and bullet holes, and I was terrified. Somehow, the motion of the car eventually made my eyelids heavy and I dozed off, leaving Mum and Dave to fire shots at each other. I woke up to Dave slamming on the brakes. All around us were paintings on the walls, paintings of men with balaclavas holding guns and the letters IRA.

'Where the bloody hell are we?' Mum screamed in Dave's ear.

I could see the fear in Dave's eyes as he studied the road map – a look I'd never seen in him before. *We're going to get shot, we're going to get shot.* I fed off his panic, my adrenalin kicking into overdrive. I clasped my seat belt so hard my fingers went numb and I closed my eyes. I never let on to Dave and Mum how scared I was; instead, I pretended to be asleep, just like when Dave hurt me.

I hoped I'd open my eyes to a magical green paradise like in the Narnia storybooks but the park in Londonderry was just as bleak as the place we'd left behind. Our caravan was perched on a cliff edge, rocking from the wind and lashing rain. It was something straight out of a horror film. I planted my feet in the grass and carefully peered over the edge to see how far the drop was.

'Oh, my God!' I wobbled, as the wind pushed into my back like a sail on a boat. I jumped backwards, terrified I was about to plunge down the cliff and be impaled on the razor-sharp rocks below.

'Flossy, stop fucking around and help Dave carry these bags!' Mum shouted as she made herself at home inside. The caravan was poky and smelt of damp, but luckily it had a bathroom unlike the ones in Clacton-on-Sea. The horrible itchy feeling had returned and it was becoming unbearable. *What's happening to my body?* I panicked and jumped into the shower hoping that would cool it down, scrubbing myself repeatedly, trying to wash away the burning itch.

I stepped out of the cupboard-sized bathroom into the

greasy smell of chip fat. We rarely went a night without chips in our family and Dave had put together a makeshift deep-fat fryer from a saucepan and oil, stinking out the tiny caravan. I was feeling so sore I didn't want to eat; I just wanted to crawl under my quilt and wake up when it was all better. Dave and Mum shared a double bed while I slept next to Jonathan. I don't know how everyone managed to get to sleep with the storm battering outside. Our feeble caravan trembled as the rain hammered the roof and the gale rattled the windows. I curled up in a ball and pulled the quilt around my ears to deafen the racket. But the noise seeped into my dreams. I squirmed in my narrow bed as I dreamt of the wind pushing the caravan to the cliff edge.

'Help!' I screamed, banging on the windows, but no sound came out of my mouth.

My head tossed violently from side to side as I imagined the caravan tipping. The rocks below had turned into a monster's teeth, the sea his saliva as he got excited about eating me.

'Help!' I woke up screaming and crying. The storm was still raging and must have drowned out my cry as no one stirred. I tried to calm myself but my skin was now so itchy there was no way I could go back to sleep. I crept to the bathroom to take another wash.

By breakfast the itching was driving me so crazy I wanted to scratch my insides out. I tried to eat my cornflakes but I couldn't sit still long enough to finish them. The rain was still pouring and the thought of all of us being stuck inside a cramped caravan while I felt like this, was too much to bear.

I was sure something nasty was festering inside me and I needed help – I had to tell Mum. The thought of talking to her about something so intimate made me squirm with embarrassment. But worse still, I'd never spoken to her about my 'injuries', and I was frightened I'd be punished for letting the cat out of the bag. I was scared, embarrassed and ashamed all at the same time and I practised in my head what I was going to say. Mum was at the sink with her back to me while Dave was out of earshot.

'Mum . . .' I started but the words caught in my throat. I was shaking.

'Mum,' I squeaked.

'What now?' she snapped

'Mum, I'm really itchy,' I started. I felt my cheeks burn red with embarrassment.

She spun round and stared at me. 'Where?' she said and frowned. We never talked about intimate things so I was lost for words.

'Down there.' I blushed, pointing.

Mum scowled and told me to leave it with her. *What did that mean? I was forever being kept in the dark. Was I sick? Did she now know about Dave?* Panic was making my emotions swing from normal to irrational to worst-case scenario.

'What's going to happen?' I whispered.

No answer. I had to wait and see. This was torture. Mum handed me a cream later that day with no explanation.

'Put that on you,' she said, without batting an eyelid. I still didn't know that what I had was thrush, a fungal infection often caused by sex; I just had to get on with it. The cream immediately soothed the burn, making our holiday just that little bit more bearable. Dave and Mum visited family that evening so I was left babysitting Jonathan. It may have been raining outside but as soon as I heard the car engine revving to go, the cloud hanging over me lifted.

'Come here, you,' I cooed, lifting Jonathan onto my knees.

'What are we going to do?' I said, nuzzling his tiny nose. His angelic blond hair and those big blue eyes staring back made me melt. I loved him like he was my own son and I could feel he loved me back. Love that no one else had ever showed me. I switched on the tiny TV and swivelled the aerial until the snow blizzard on the screen disappeared.

'Cartoons – you like them, don't you?' I said, snuggling us under my quilt.

'Don't be scared of the storm. I'll protect you,' I promised, cuddling him.

I didn't know who was going to protect me though.

But I was finally accepting I wouldn't be saved.

9

Fight for Your Life

Half of the school had snuck to the park at lunchtime to watch the fight. Lisa Long had been my friend when we lived in Maygreen Crescent but now she was my enemy. She'd joined Frances Bardsley School late, in our second year, and I felt she was my rival. She'd thrown some catty insult at me about my mum being fat and I needed to show her who was boss. The news that we'd be having a fight spread around school like wildfire and one after the other the girls climbed through the hole in the fence into Highlands Park behind our classrooms.

'C'mon then,' Lisa chanted, riling up our audience, who had formed a boxing ring around us.

'C'mon then,' I beckoned with my hands.

But neither of us wanted to throw the first punch, so the girls pushed us into it. I flew forward and slapped her across the face. She tumbled back onto her bum and everyone gasped. I watched with excitement as her eyes narrowed and she charged for me like a rocket.

'C'mon, Tina,' the girls screamed. No one would dare cross me by supporting the new girl.

'Hit her,' they chanted.

Lisa battered me with slaps around the face and the head but I was bigger and stronger than her. And no one was a match for the anger that raged inside of me. I grabbed her hair with both hands and pulled as hard as I could.

'*Owwwww*,' she screamed, as I took away clumps.

I forced her down, using her hair to bang her head on the concrete. I was like a girl posessed. She was now a rag doll being tossed around.

'Tina stop, you'll kill her!' one of the girls screamed. But I kept going until Lisa sunk her teeth into my arm.

'You bitch!' I cried out. The monster inside had now exploded through my skin. I went for her again with the force of years of pent-up anger. The girls pulled us apart as they could see things had turned dangerous.

'Get off me!' I shouted, thrashing my arms around. That was the first serious fight I'd got into, which gave me even more of a tough-nut reputation.

As I wiped the blood from my bite mark, I thought about what Dave had done to me the night before . . .

He'd come into my bedroom as usual, he'd pulled down my knickers, as usual, but then he'd stopped and walked out again, and not shut the door. I froze as I realised he'd broken the ritual and I was in for something painful.

I heard him root around in the bathroom, opening and closing the cabinet. I could only guess what apparatus he was going to bring with him this time. I lay there like a patient on an operating table, waiting for the doctor to do what he wanted with me, only I wasn't under anaesthetic, *I could feel everything*.

Something cold touched the outside of my private area. Something cold and scraping in an upward motion over my skin. A chill ran down my spine.

'That feels really nice, really smooth,' he drooled, stroking between my legs with his clammy fingers.

Dave then clambered on top and raped me. As soon as he left I examined the damage – my stepdad had shaved the tiny bit of hair that had grown down there. I didn't understand why. I didn't want to know why . . .

I looked a mess as we walked into afternoon classes but Lisa looked worse. She had a gash across her forehead and her hair was a tangled bird's nest. Strangely, no teachers questioned me about my aggressive behaviour inside and outside the classroom. They just chucked a bit of chalk at my head when they wanted me to shut up.

I'd also started to question how it was strange that Dave never asked me to keep 'our secret' a secret. I was thirteen and, although I played dumb in class to get attention, I had a brain on me. When I wasn't trying to forget, questions would whir around in my head. *Was my stepdad not scared I would tell my friends? Was he so confident that he knew I was too terrified to talk? Or was he living in fear just like me?*

I was making it harder for him to buy my silence. I stopped wanting to go shopping with him on Saturdays because I'd rather get away from my family and smoke down the park with my friends. I wanted cigarettes, not a can of hairspray or a bottle of mousse. I guess that's why Dave found another way to get under my skin. One night after he had raped me, he paused by my bedside and placed something on my table.

'I've left you some money for being a good girl,' he whispered. I could imagine his lips snaking up into a smile.

As soon as he'd gone, I pulled my bedclothes back on and hid under my protective quilt before finally peeping at what he'd left behind – it was a £10 note. It was the most money I'd seen other than the notes Mum handed me to get her fags and booze from the shop. I couldn't bring myself to touch it though – it was like a poison apple – too good to be true. I could feel the note burn next to me as I tried to sleep, weighing down on my conscience. I eventually rolled over and slipped it into my drawer with all my other gifts.

I woke up to a war zone. Jonathan was crying, Mum was yelling and Dave was charging down the corridor with a knife.

'This is the last fucking time you'll be late for school,' he threatened. The knife edge glistened and I slammed my door, terrified.

He's going to kill Blake. I panicked, barring my door with my back.

'You fucking lazy cunt!' he shouted, charging into Blake and Jonathan's bedroom.

'I'm getting ready,' Blake pleaded. Jonathan was screaming. I wanted to rescue him but my legs had turned to jelly.

'No more TV for you,' he said, and then the background noise went dead.

'You bastard,' Blake hissed.

'What did you say?' spat Dave. WHACK, WHACK, WHACK.

Then everything went dead. Not even a cry from Jonathan. I felt light-headed as I imagined a room full of blood and guts. I was now constantly in a state of fight-or-flight with the amount of adrenalin that was kicking around in my body. I heard Dave stomp downstairs and I peeped out to see the carnage. Jonathan was hiding under his quilt, Blake was hobbling, and the TV lead in his room was now only a few centimetres long where Dave had cut it so many times. Blake flashed me a look of hate and slammed his door in my face.

I went back into my room and pulled the £10 out of my drawer. Dave's rage had scared me again and with that came a crash in confidence. *I could use this money to buy some fags and sweets for my mates. That way I'll make sure I won't end up alone without friends again.* I pushed the note into my bag and ran out the door before anyone could shout at me.

Eight out of ten times my stepdad raped me, he would leave money by my bedside table, anything from £5 to £30. If he didn't, he'd whisper that he'd give it to me another time, as long as I let him touch me. He spoke to me like I had a choice, like we were having a conversation. But I didn't have any choice, he would have done it anyway, he had been for all those years. Dave always kept to his promise and left a note under my quilt the following day.

The money threw me into even more turmoil because I became dependent on it, on him, to keep my friends. Being the bad girl who gave away cigarettes had made me very popular and I'd get nauseous at the thought of losing all that attention to become Miss Nobody again. Being able to mess around with my friends like a normal child should was one of the few things that helped me forget the pain 'down there' for minutes at a time. I was too young to realise, but Dave had cunningly led me into a wicked cycle of abuse.

The pain after sex had turned worse, since I'd stopped hearing a packet being unwrapped before he forced into me. There was now an ache deep inside that felt like someone was stirring my organs around with a big wooden spoon. I was still too scared to tell Mum about Dave but I tried to show her. I came to her with my latest injury, desperate for her love and attention.

'Mum, my period is really hurting me,' I cried.

'Periods can be painful,' Mum dismissed me.

'But, Mum, I'm in agony,' I exaggerated, bending double in pain.

'What can I fucking do about it? Go and lie down,' she ordered. I crawled up to my room, whining, hoping she'd take pity on me. It took two days of groaning and crying for her to eventually take notice and she drove me to the gynaecologist unit at Rush Green Hospital. I was so happy to have her all to myself again, just like the time I'd faked my sprained ankle, that I didn't stop to think what this check-up would entail.

A lady doctor with dark hair tied neatly into a high bun led us into a small room, where she sat me down on a plastic chair opposite her.

'I've got tummy pain,' I mumbled. I watched her eyes flash across to Mum and I suddenly became aware of the seriousness of the situation.

'I'm going to have to examine you,' she said. *Examination? She must mean lift up my T-shirt and look at my tummy. Why's the doctor looking so serious about that?*

We were led into a huge room with cream walls, which had a single bed in the centre with two strange metal arms sticking out. I looked back at Mum, but her eyes had already turned into emotionless marble. The doctor handed me a green gown and pulled the curtain around so I could get changed in privacy. I had to take all my clothes off, which I hated doing because that's what *he* liked to do to me. I slipped the massive gown over my head, leaving the ties at the back. I nervously pulled back the curtain and edged forward into the giant room. The green gown drowned my little body and I pinned the gaping hole in the back with my hand while the doctor beckoned me to come forward.

'Sit back and put your legs in either stirrup,' she instructed, while Mum took a seat at the head of the bed. I hitched myself up onto the steel bed and manoeuvred my legs into the robotic-looking arms, exposing my private parts.

'This is going to feel a bit cold but try and relax,' she said softly.

I felt a sharp pain as something cold and hard was inserted into me. It was just like when *he* stuck that cold vibrating object inside me. I examined the grey-cream ceiling with its cracked and peeling paint, and started to cry.

'You're being a very brave girl,' the doctor said soothingly as she widened the object and started scraping inside me.

Tears streamed down my face as I remembered all the

horrible things my stepdad liked to do to me. I hated him touching me and now I was in a huge, lonely room, with my legs wide open in a position he often left me in, with a stranger fishing around inside me. I was sobbing and wailing so hard even my mum had to step in.

'I know it's horrible but when you have kids you won't care when people are looking up you down there,' she said matter-of-factly, with no heart, no emotion.

Oh, that makes me feel a thousand times better, I thought as I lay there in agony. The examination felt like it went on for hours but eventually the doctor stopped and pulled the metal thing out.

'OK, all over, you can get dressed now,' she said calmly. I snaked my arms across my chest protectively and hobbled behind the curtain, tears still streaming down my face. I think it was the first time I'd allowed myself to really cry in front of someone and I felt exhausted but better for getting all the poison out.

The doctor had that serious look on her face again as she ushered my mum into the small room with her and I waited outside on the plastic chair. I watched the doctors rush past and the second hand of the clock go round – *tick tock*.

Tick tock.

Mum came out with a grave expression on her face as if someone had told her I'd died.

'What?' I gasped.

She thrust some antibiotics and painkillers in my lap.

'You've got pelvic inflammatory disease,' she said, irritated and agitated.

'What's that?' I asked. I should have known better than to ask for an explanation.

Mum ignored my question and bulldozed on to say how often I needed to swallow the pills. She hurried me to the car and I was left wandering what was wrong with my insides, again.

She was quiet the whole way back and looked in deep thought as we curled around the roads to our council estate. Pelvic inflammatory disease sounded serious, and I was on medication. I smiled as I realised the potential to milk my illness for attention. Little did I know that the condition was often caused through catching a sexually transmitted disease. How would I have known that? The doctor had told Mum, not me.

I walked through the door, clutching my stomach, and Blake rolled his eyes with jealousy. Mum told me to lie down and she would come up with a drink in a while. I was in heaven.

I bunked off school for the next couple of days with my partner in crime, Sam Aitken, because I thought my illness deserved a bit of time off. We sat in the park, smoking and talking about everything except what Dave liked to do to me. I didn't tell her I was on antibiotics because I would then have to explain about the internal examination, which was too embarrassing. Instead, I joked and messed around like any thirteen-year-old would.

'Who can jump the furthest off the swings?' I challenged Sam as we raced each other to the kid's playground. I launched myself into the air and built up the momentum, swinging back and forth, up and higher. I may have been flying but something in the pit of my stomach was weighing me down like lead. I was near breaking point and I didn't know how much longer I could go on.

'*Whoopeeee*,' I shrieked as I torpedoed through the air, crashing onto the playground carpet.

'You're nuts,' Sam gasped through her gappy front teeth.

I'd torn the skin off both my knees and elbows but pain didn't frighten me any more. I was losing the will to live.

Dave didn't come near me for a while. *Did Mum tell him I had this pelvic inflammatory disease? Did they ever discuss me?* They liked to laugh and get drunk with their new friends from across the road though. They were playing Queen CDs until the early hours and I could hear the bottles and glasses clanking against the coffee table. Sue had an annoying laugh like a hyena and I wished she would shut up. I couldn't have drifted off long before I smelt Dave's boozy breath and Old Spice wafting over me.

'If you're a good girl and let me play with you, I'll leave you some money,' he slurred, coughing his phlegm over my face. He answered for me and clambered up, resting on his heels at the end of my bed. I felt cold under his glare. I could imagine him staring at my body, his eyes running over every curve and roll of puppy fat.

'Relax,' he whispered, forcing my legs apart. He raped me slowly this time as if he knew I'd been on medication.

When he left, I had to hurt myself to be able to get to sleep. SMACK, SMACK, SMACK – I punched my legs. He must have seen the damage on my legs – they were a kaleidoscope of blue and purple and yellow from the weeks of battering. I rolled off my bed and crouched on the floor, resting my elbows on my mattress. I clasped my hands together and begged for mercy.

'Please, please, please, God, please make him stop,' I prayed.

'I can't go on any more.'

10

Caught Red-Handed

My screaming fights with my mum were getting worse by the day.

'I hate you, I wish you were dead!' I yelled. Now I was the one making the walls of the house shake. Mum laughed in my face, which made me ten times angrier, and a thousand times sadder. I didn't hate her because she had grounded me again – the real reason I couldn't bear to look at her any more was because she refused to save me from my life of rape and abuse. Whether she couldn't, or wouldn't, see what was going on under her nose, I could only conclude that she didn't love me enough.

But every time I hated her, the fighter inside made me work harder to make her love me, make her notice me – so she would eventually come to my rescue.

I crouched down on the dirty bathroom floor and inspected the thick layer of grime and limescale that had built up over the year that we had been living in Rush Green. I pulled out an old toothbrush and started scrubbing. Round and around the bath taps and sink hole until I could see my reflection. My hands were wrinkly and shrivelled but two hours later our bathroom looked like something straight out of a show home.

'Ta daaaa!' I said to myself, as I stood up and admired my handiwork. 'Mum will have to love me for doing this,' I muttered, sweeping one last polish of the tiles.

'BANG BANG . . .' It was Mum rapping on the door. I knew it was her from the sound of her fist.

'What the fuck are you doing in there? I need the toilet!' she shouted.

I wanted to savour the moment, so I slowly unlocked the door and stood back.

'Fuckin hell, Flossy,' Mum gasped.

'Who said I couldn't clean?' I beamed.

'Since you did such a good job, you can do this every week,' Mum said, before charging in, shoving me out and slamming the door in my face. I'd been thrown a scrap of thanks but it was the most I could have hoped for, and I glowed inside as the candle of hope reignited.

I cooked, I cleaned, I baked cakes, I did everything I could to make her love me. And when I wasn't trying to win her approval I made myself scarce to avoid her blows and not anger her. I wanted her love so badly that the mum I wished I had would visit me in my dreams. I'd often wake up swimming in sweat, my head feeling light like a helium balloon and my chest, tight, like an elephant was sitting on it. I'd dream I was buried alive in the same glass coffin I always imagined, being fed air by a tiny tube, but this time I'd have a lighter by my side to see the worms and woodlice crawling around me . . .

I'd bang, and scream, but no one could hear me.

'Help, someone save me!' I yelled, pounding the glass with my fists, but no one can hear me. I've been left to slowly starve to death in what I suddenly realised was my back garden. Just as I'm giving up, a light appears above me where nails are clawing through the earth like a shovel. I recognise those hands.

'*Muuuuum!*' I scream.

'Help me, Mum, I'm trapped,' I rasp, thumping, kicking, punching the glass as hard as I can. Mum is looking worried as she claws at the earth, clearing a hole to where my face is. I'm looking right up at her but she can't see me in the coffin. I watch in horror as she clears more soil away but shakes her head in defeat.

'It's empty,' she says and turns to the dark shadow that is looming behind her.

'Noooooo, Mum, I'm here.' I bang on the top of the coffin. She lifts herself off her knees and kicks the earth back over me.

'Look at me, I'm here!' I scream, but the air catches in my throat and no sound comes out. The lighter burns out and I'm left in darkness, to die. And then I wake up . . .

The dreams were so traumatic I would often carry them with me through my day at school. The girls caught me on one of my dark days when they persuaded me to join them with their Ouija board to evoke the spirits. I was already in hell, how much more scary could life get? Five of us held hands as we sat cross-legged on the floor in our form room near the science block. It was raining April showers outside, sending the humidity in the room soaring, and my fingers were tacky with sweat. We'd made a makeshift board with the letters of the alphabet, numbers one to nine and the words YES and NO on a piece of ruled notepaper. Our planchette was someone's grubby sharpener they had dusted off from their pencil case. We all placed our forefingers on the sharpener and Mel asked the first question.

'Spirits, we call out to you. Do you hear us?' she asked, deliberately making her voice tremble.

The others sniggered and told her to stop messing around.

'That's not how you do it, you idiot,' I butted in.

'Go on then, know it all, show us,' Mel taunted.

'Are there any spirits with us in this room?' I asked. We all fell silent and looked at each other, waiting for something to happen. After ten seconds the sharpener started to move across the notepad.

'*Owwwoooooooooo,*' everyone chanted as our fingers were pushed across the page to the word YES. The girls let out a gasp but Sarah couldn't contain her mischief any longer and burst out laughing, spraying everyone with her giggles.

'Sarah, you idiot.' I told her off for moving the sharpener. We quickly lost interest in our séance after that and the conversation turned to boys – something I wasn't comfortable speaking about at all.

One of the girls, who had an older boyfriend who was a mechanic, boasted that she had done everything but have sex with him.

'I touched his willy the other night.' She blushed, sending

the other girls into fits of giggles. My face turned to stone as I was reminded of how dirty I was.

'It was big and hard and looked freaky.' She laughed, showing us with her hands.

I squirmed in my seat. *Shut up shut up*.

'Has anyone had sex?' she asked.

The colour drained from my face as the other girls let out gasps of innocence. I bowed my head to make sure no one read my guilt.

'Sex is for grown-ups. I'm not "doing it" until I get married,' one of the more geeky girls chastised us and the others booed her for being boring. I'd started the day feeling out of sorts thanks to my nightmare and I returned home feeling even worse.

I stomped straight to my bedroom so I could lie on my bed and listen to music until I had to make dinner. I threw my green school uniform onto the floor and slipped under my quilt. *What's this?* I felt something cold and flat jabbing into my back. I sat up and pulled out two magazines that had pictures of naked women on the front. I had no idea they were porn; I was only thirteen. I innocently flicked through one of the magazines and was horrified at the graphic images. Women's boobs, close-up shots of women's vaginas. I LIKE IT HARD was branded above a woman bent on all-fours.

'*Eugh*.' I shivered. I slammed the pages shut in disgust and tucked the magazines under my bed so they were hidden by the valance sheet. There was no question about who had left them there; the question was why my stepdad wanted me to see them.

As usual I didn't have to wait long for my answer. I couldn't fall asleep that night because I knew I would be getting a visitor. My body was tense and rigid even before he creaked open my door. He tiptoed up to my bed and I could smell his unwashed groin in my face. I wanted to gag. Dave pushed me onto my back and did his usual tug of war with my PJs. He then smothered his fingers in the creamy pot and massaged the goo between my legs, up my legs, spread my legs, and thrust more than one finger into me.

'You're really sexy,' he whispered as he played inside me.

'I want to take some pictures of you,' he groaned.

'You could earn a lot of money from it,' he went on, thrusting in and out of me. *Stop, it hurts, stop. Please stop.*

'You just have to let me take your picture,' he whispered again as if we were having a conversation.

He pulled his fingers out and I had a moment to recover while he slipped his pants off and clambered on top of me. I'd pushed my legs back together but he carried on as if they were open. He thrust until he punctured me and then built up his momentum.

'Just put the magazines back where they were before, if you're all right with it,' he dribbled in my ear.

'I'll let you have the money,' he groaned, stabbing me deeper until he was done with me.

I never left those magazines where he told me to leave them. I didn't understand what sort of pictures he wanted to take of me and why, but I could just tell it was for very bad things. I'd pretended I was asleep for all those years, I wasn't about to wake up and pose for the camera for him, no matter how much money he was offering me. The Tina he touched in the night was a corpse as far as I was concerned. The next time I looked under my bed the magazines had gone and Dave didn't mention them again.

It was music to my ears when Dave and Mum announced they were leaving Blake and I home alone for the weekend while they flew to Ireland to sort out some things with Dave's family. A boulder had been lifted off my shoulders, as I didn't have to watch my back for a whole three nights and two days.

'Don't burn the place down, no friends round, and for fuck's sake, no fighting with your brother,' Mum snarled as she handed her suitcase to Dave to carry to the car.

'All right, all right.' I nodded, barely able to contain my excitement. I closed the front door after them and punched the air with my fists. I nose-dived for the sofa and grabbed the controller as I landed. I'd snuggled into the imprint Mum's big bum had left behind and flicked through the channels, seeing if there were some cartoons I could watch. Blake's ears must have pricked up at the sound of the front door slamming and he plodded down the stairs with a glint of troublemaking in his eye.

I narrowed my eyes as if to say don't come anywhere near me and his top lip lifted into a snarl. He was ten months older but I was bigger than him now and we looked nothing like each other. He had a mop of blond hair that he liked to shake out of his eyes, whereas my mane was dark chestnut and it had grown so long it now tumbled down my back. He hated that I had beaten him to the TV and stuck the knife in.

'I'm sleeping in Mum and Dad's double bed tonight,' he announced.

'No, you're not,' I reacted, my hackles rising.

'Yes, I am, Tina,' he spat sarcastically.

'No, you're not, I'm sleeping there because I need to use Mum's alarm clock,' I retaliated, rising to my feet. I'd just started a paper round and I didn't have my own alarm to wake me at the crack of dawn.

'Ha, no, you're not,' Blake cackled, racing upstairs. I charged after him like a bull but he was quicker, and locked their bedroom door behind him, leaving me crashing into the door.

I turned mad with rage. I thumped, kicked, punched the door violently, just like when I was trapped in my glass coffin. I screamed, I swore; I wanted to kill him.

'I'm going to get you, you little shit!' I yelled through the door. He'd destroyed my one hope of a peaceful weekend without abuse. I hated him with all my heart.

'Calm the fuck down,' Blake's voice trembled.

'DON'T TELL ME TO CALM DOWN!' I screamed at the top of my voice. I kicked the door so hard my foot went through it. I was so possessed I didn't even feel it, but the gaping hole stopped me in my tracks.

'Oh, shit,' I muttered, as it dawned on me what I'd done. I backed off and let myself cool down, as Blake remained barricaded in Mum's room.

'Mum is going to KILL you,' he said. His taunt would have been enough to set me off again if the fear of Mum's beating hadn't already sunk in. I retreated to my bedroom and sat on my bed; my heart was like a hammer thumping through my chest. We kept out of each other's way for the rest of the weekend but the dark shadow of fear hung over me the whole time and I didn't get to relax and enjoy my holiday.

I nearly jumped out of my skin when I heard the front door slam and Jonathan's squeaks as he toddled after Mum and Dave into the living room.

Oh, God, they're back, I'm in for it now.

A few seconds later the TV was back blasting out *Knots Landing*, Mum's latest favourite soap opera. I'd already prepared dinner to butter them up but Blake couldn't wait a second longer to stick his oar in.

'Tina's kicked a hole in your bedroom door,' he sang like a canary.

'What?' Dave barked.

'I'll go and fucking look,' Mum sighed. I scrambled back to my bedroom from my peeping hole at the top of the stairs and waited for the scream. I could hear my heart in my ears.

Ba-boom Ba-boom. Nothing yet.

Ba-boom. Still no yell. I edged my way out to see what was holding Mum up. She was standing in her familiar skirt and sandals with her hands on both hips.

'I'm sorry, Mum, but Blake wouldn't let me in the room,' I mumbled. She sighed deeply and then turned her marble eyes on me.

'Well, at least you didn't set the house on fire.' She shrugged.

The rug had been pulled from beneath my feet, again. I just never knew where I stood with her. I frowned with disbelief. I almost would have preferred a beating because then I could relax. She must have had a good holiday with Dave, I decided, as I scurried back to my den.

I was just regaining a tiny bit of confidence in my mum when she failed me more than she's ever failed me. She took me to a point of no return.

It was a night like so many of the hundreds of others. I'd lost count of how many times my stepdad had crept into my room in the dead of night; to me it had become one long continuous rape. I had nearly turned fourteen and Dave was crouched by my side, preparing me with his fingers and creams.

'Ooooh, you feel so nice,' he groaned, as he played with himself.

'You'll enjoy this,' he promised me, as he rose to his feet.

CLUNK.

We both froze.

Dave pulled up his pants and darted across my pink carpet to the door, as he realised my mum had woken up and was walking around. She had gone to the bathroom, and he had only a tiny window to get out without being caught. He was just closing my door behind him when I heard:

'What you doing?' My mum had caught him red-handed.

He carried on closing my door behind him and I couldn't hear the rest of their conversation no matter how hard I strained my ears. My heart hammered again, but this time

Tina Renton

with happiness, as I realised it was over. It was finally over. I WAS FREE.

I couldn't sleep a wink as I was half expecting Mum to charge into my room that night like a knight on a white steed, scoop me up and carry me somewhere far away where I would be safe for the rest of my life.

'I'm sorry, Flossy,' she would say to me. The three words I'd been most longing to hear after 'I love you'. I'd look her in the eyes and enjoy the moment of watching her squirm as she hung on my every word. And then I'd say, 'I forgive you' because at the end of the day, no matter what she's done, she's still my mum.

Tears of happiness rolled down my cheeks as I imagined her hugging me for the first time and reassuring me that everything was going to be OK. I grabbed my pillow and squeezed that instead, as I waited for Mum to come through for me. I must have dozed off sitting upright in bed, since I woke up with a very stiff neck and the sunshine streaming through my curtains.

I reluctantly scraped myself out of bed for school as usual; but as I reached my door, I remembered the drama of last night. *Mum had caught you leaving my room. How you gonna get yourself out of that, Dave?* However big and tough I'd made myself at school, I suddenly reverted to Tina the child who was petrified that her stepdad would beat the crap out of her now the cat was out of the bag. *Should I go downstairs for breakfast as normal?* I popped my head around the door to hear the kettle boiling and the clang of breakfast bowls coming from the kitchen.

Blake was slurping the last dribbles of milk from his cereal bowl and Jonathan was thumping his spoon on the table. Luckily Dave had already gone out on one of his delivery jobs, so I had Mum all to myself before she left for work at the solicitor's in town.

'Cereal or toast?' she asked.

I was so gobsmacked I couldn't speak. This wasn't how I'd imagined it to go. *Shouldn't you be asking me what your husband was doing in my room last night? Shouldn't you be apologising to me for not protecting me?*

'What?' She shrugged as I stared at her.

'Cereal,' I whispered. I didn't have any voice left.

She placed the box of cornflakes on the table and carried on feeding Jonathan, like nothing had happened, like nothing had changed. The candle of hope inside my chest flickered, and blew out.

Enough Is Enough

Everyone has their breaking point, even the strongest, bravest warriors. I'd reached mine but I just didn't quite know it yet. Our annual summer trip to Highfields in Clacton-on-Sea, when I turned fourteen, was a far cry from my memories of belly-flopping off the ginormous diving board and playing on the arcade machines. They were never happy memories but this time around my week passed as a blur.

I couldn't bear to watch Mum and Dave frolic around like they didn't have a care in the world, while my stomach was eating me up from inside. I wanted to block out all the pain. I needed to numb my entire body like I was under anaesthetic. So I did what they did – I reached for the bottle.

'You couldn't get me a bottle of Martini, could you?' I asked some of the older kids who were hanging around outside the off-licence near the caravan park. I held out a crumpled £10 note, which my stepdad had left for raping me.

'I'll give you some smokes for doing me a favour,' I promised, as they looked me up and down. One of the lads went into the shop and came out carrying a thin plastic blue carrier.

'Don't drink it all at once,' he smirked, handing it over to me.

I glanced at him through the greasy straggles of hair hiding my face.

'Thanks,' I muttered, too shy to look him in the eyes. I was dressed head to foot in loose-fitting clothes to hide every inch of the body I'd come to hate.

The sun was setting and the sound of the other holiday-makers could be heard the closer I got to the club house. Sunburnt families were walking back to their vans carrying armfuls of buckets and spades and stripy windbreaks. The ice-cream van came every evening at 5 p.m. singing its annoying song but I didn't want a Mr Whippy, I wanted to get off my face drunk so I couldn't even remember my name.

I checked over my shoulder to see if anyone was watching, then I snuck behind the back of the club house. The concrete was still scorching hot from a day baking in the sun but the burn on my bum died down after a few minutes. I unscrewed the lid of the bottle and took a giant glug.

'*Eugh*,' I spluttered, spraying it everywhere. The bitter liquid burnt my throat.

I thought about Mum and Dave and our neighbours, Tony and Sue, who were having fun in the club behind me. I raised the bottle into a toast and took another giant glug.

Half a bottle later, I was paralytic. I was sprawled across the concrete and I couldn't feel my limbs.

'Tina?' I heard my name.

'Tina, are you drunk?' The man's voice echoed between my ears. I remember rolling over and looking up at Tony, who was wearing a loud Hawaiian shirt. He scooped me up into his arms and I told him I was going to be sick. Next thing I remember is lying on a bed in a caravan, but not our van, as it had a differently coloured flowery curtain and garish bed sheets.

'You can sleep it off here, so you don't get into trouble with Mum and Dave,' Tony said. I was drunk but I'll never forget the pity in his eyes. He stared at me for a few seconds longer, then closed the door behind him.

I don't know if it was the family holiday in Highfields or just the gloomy rainy weather that was the final straw. I was with my friend Sam, who also liked to bunk off school. We had taken the morning off, but our plan to go boating on the lake in Barking Park had been rained off, so we headed to the library in Romford for shelter.

I jumped up the stairs two at a time, to the first floor where we would be out the way of the eagle-eyed librarian. The humid weather had brought out the smell of old books, which didn't mix well with the stench of the same cleaning fluid they used to wipe the tables in school. I pulled out the fattest book I could find and slammed it open on the plastic-topped table. Sam did the same and we giggled at how naughty we were being.

'You're into Dickens now, are ya?!' Sam sniggered at my book.

'Shhhh,' I said, holding my finger to my mouth. 'You'll get us chucked out of here.'

Sam pulled a face as she swept her blonde boyish haircut out of her eyes.

'I'm not going to be around this weekend because we are going for a family trip to Brighton. Dad said he's going to take me up the pier and we're going to try out the new roller coaster,' she said, beaming.

Her words were like a javelin through my heart. Why don't I do things like that? All I wanted was a normal family life. I'd had enough.

'My life is nothing like yours,' I said, stony-faced.

'Whad'ya mean?' she chuckled.

'My stepdad touches me.'

'What do ya mean, he touches ya?' She laughed, thinking I was cracking some sick joke.

'He touches me,' I whispered, looking down at the book. 'He touches me. He comes in my room and he has sex with me.' I looked her in the eye. My voice was trembling.

Sam's mouth dropped open. 'Have you just said what I think you've just said?' she gasped.

The elephant that had been sitting on my chest for the past eight years since Dave first started touching me had finally got off and let me breathe.

'What are you going to do about it?' she asked, still gobsmacked.

'I'm not gonna do anything about it,' I said. I hadn't planned to tell Sam, it had just blurted out of my mouth as if I'd been violently sick.

'But you've got to tell someone,' she hissed, leaning across the table.

I lurched back in horror at the thought. 'I can't, I can't,' I said, shaking my head. But Sam wouldn't give up.

'We're going to go back to school and you need to tell a teacher,' she insisted. After all those years of abuse, I think I was still numb to how serious what Dave had done to me really was.

'Hell, no, no way,' I said, standing up. Sam tried to plead with me but I wasn't ready to tell the world what he had done. I was ashamed, disgusted with myself.

We had to go back to school for afternoon registration so we wouldn't be caught bunking off. It was just our luck that we were caught sneaking up the drive.

'Miss Moore, Miss Aitken, where do you think you've been?' bellowed the stern voice of Mrs Walsh, our head of year. I hated her because she was always the teacher I was sent to for detention.

'Oh, God, we're in for it now,' I muttered to Sam as Mrs Walsh stood arms folded, tapping her foot impatiently on the tarmac. She was tall but had a big bum. Her shoulder-length hair parted like a curtain but then flicked up at the bottom. She had the look of death and Sam and I were scared. She glared down at us through her long eyelashes, which looked like spiders' legs because they were glued together with thick black mascara.

'Tina's got something to tell you, Miss,' Sam piped up.

'Shut up, shut up,' I hissed, nudging Sam in the ribs.

'No, you've got to tell her. Either you do or I will,' she insisted, pushing me forward.

I was on a runaway train and didn't know how to make it

stop. My confession to Sam in the library had snowballed to a size I never wanted it to become. I hadn't been able to catch my breath and think where it would all lead.

'My stepdad's been touching me,' I mumbled. My cheeks burnt with shame.

Mrs Walsh didn't need me to spell it out to her twice. She puffed out her chest like an angry cockerel and jabbed out her finger.

'Right, you,' she said, pointing at me, 'and you', pointing at Sam, 'follow me. Say nothing more.' She turned and charged up the drive, with us cantering to keep up with her. She left Sam sitting in the reception while she led me into her office. She closed the door behind us and the blinds clanged against the glass.

She pointed to the seat opposite her as she mounted her throne behind her desk. Finally her steel look melted as she took pity on me. She smiled through her eyes and asked if I was OK. I nodded, nervously playing with the pleats on my skirt. The ticking clock above her desk sounded like a hammer as we sat in awkward silence for a moment.

'So, what do you mean, he's been touching you?' she said. It was strange hearing the *nice* Mrs Walsh.

'He comes into my bedroom in the night.' I cringed, running one thumbnail under the other.

'Where does he touch you?' she asked, sweetly.

The air caught in my throat again and I couldn't speak.

'It's OK,' she reassured me.

I took another deep breath and told her where he liked to use his fingers. How often he raped me. That it started when

I was six years old. I didn't cry because it still didn't feel real. It was like I was having an out-of-body experience, robotically listing the facts and figures for her. We were in her office for a long time and, strangely, I felt more love coming from Mrs Walsh than I'd ever felt from my mum.

'What time is it?' she muttered to herself as she looked at her watch. 'It's nearly the end of the school day, so I need you to go home, and I need you to tell your mum what has been happening,' she said to me, her face looking serious again.

I let out a gasp of horror. *Tell my mum? She must be joking.* 'I can't,' I said, shaking my head from side to side.

'You've got to, Tina, it's the only way to stop this,' she insisted, leaning across the desk. I nodded but wasn't sure if I meant it.

'Come see me first thing tomorrow and tell me how it went,' Mrs Walsh ordered as I was leaving her office. I nodded again, still unsure whether I had the guts to follow through. I got the bus home with all the other girls from school but I didn't say a word to any of them. I was too busy rehearsing what I was going to say to Mum. *Mum, Dave's been having sex with me.* No, I can't say it like that. *Mum, your husband likes to stick things inside me.* No way could I say that. I felt myself turn angry as I thought about all the pain he had put me through.

'Come on, you can do it, Tina,' the fighter in me snapped as I walked up our drive. I knew Mum was already home from work, as I could smell the chip fat wafting into our front garden. My heart cantered as I turned the handle and then it exploded into a gallop as I saw Mum in the kitchen with her back to me.

Ba-boom ba-boom ba-boom.

I turned around for the stairs to my room. 'No, Tina, SAY IT!' The voice in my head stopped me fleeing. I spun on my heels and charged for her.

'Mum,' I said.

She carried on preparing the food.

'Mum, I need to talk to you,' I said even louder. She slammed down the plates and turned to face her annoying daughter. I took a deep breath ...

... and then Dave walked in.

'Well, what do you need to talk to me about?' she barked.

I looked at Dave and shook my head. 'It doesn't matter,' I said and went up my room. I was determined not to give up though; Miss Walsh made me promise. I waited until Mum was upstairs watching TV alone in bed to give it a second shot. I hovered by her doorway and then plunged in.

'Mum, can I talk to you?' I started.

'Mummy, Mummy, look at this ...' Jonathan came running in, clutching a toy.

'You know what, it doesn't matter,' I sighed, retreating back into the hallway. I lay on my bed for hours that night, almost relieved that I hadn't blurted it out. *I can't do it, I don't know how to. How can I possibly tell her what he's doing?* A big part of me felt guilty, thinking I was somehow to blame. I accepted those gifts. I accepted the money. I didn't tell him NO. But above all, I didn't want to upset my mum, because despite everything, I wanted to please her and make her happy. *How could I burden her with the truth?*

I went into school the next morning with a big 'F' for 'Failed' for Mrs Walsh. 'I couldn't do it, I couldn't tell her,' I whimpered, wrapping my arms across my chest as I sat in her office. Mrs Walsh brushed her hair off her shoulder and stared me right in the eye.

'The only way this will stop, Tina, is if you tell your mum,' she said sternly, grinding her palms together. Her spider-leg lashes were looking longer than ever that morning. It's funny what you focus on when you feel under the spotlight. She then took her finger off the pressure and told me I would be spending the day with her until it was time to go home and face my mum again.

That Friday was one of the best days I'd ever spent at school. Mrs Walsh took me under her wing and never let me out of her sight. I felt protected and wanted and needed. A feeling I had yearned for my whole childhood. I sat through all her lessons and would help her out, fetching her whistle from the classroom. It was finally starting to sink in that something major had changed in my life and I felt incredibly relieved that I had told her.

'I want you to come and see me first thing on Monday,' she made me promise again as the last bell for the week drilled through the corridors and classrooms. I could tell she didn't want to let me go, as her smile crinkled into a concerned frown.

'You'll be OK,' she said, and I nodded. I didn't want to leave her side, I felt safe and protected. As soon as I made my way home alone my body temperature dropped as if I'd stepped away from a warm homely fire into a blizzard outside. I shivered as I opened the front door. Thank God, Mum wasn't there – I had a few more minutes to prepare myself. I was even more nervous than yesterday, as I'd built the confession into a massive drama in my head.

I lay on my bed and waited for her to come home from work. Blake was downstairs watching TV and I could hear the *Doctor Who* theme tune blaring. I was lying down but not resting – that horrible in-between feeling that makes you even more exhausted than if you'd been walking around.

The door went.

Deep breath.

I heard her knock her sandals off under the peg rail in the hall, and then the creaking of the stairs.

Another deep breath. I heard her go into her bedroom and open up her closet. It was now or never. Mum was sitting on the edge of their double bed when I walked in still wearing my school uniform. I was terrified, my hands were shaking, my legs were giddy like a newborn calf – one push and I would have toppled like a house of cards.

'I want to talk to you,' I announced. I had no choice, Mrs Walsh had threatened that if I didn't, she'd be ringing my mum on Monday.

'What about?' she asked. I walked over and sat a few feet from her on the edge of the bed. *Their bed, which he crawls into after raping me.*

'Dave has been touching me,' I blurted out.

Silence.

Mum then screwed up her face like she hadn't understood properly. 'What?' she said, and frowned.

'He's been touching me?' I repeated.

'What do you mean?' she asked, narrowing her eyes.

'Coming in my room at night,' I mumbled, hanging my head in shame.

A stream of red moved from her neck up to her cheeks and she looked like she was about to cry.

'What's he been doing to you?' she asked, obviously scared about what I was going to tell her.

I gulped another deep breath. Mum and I never talked about the birds and the bees, so I felt very uncomfortable describing any abuse in detail.

'He's been touching my ... my private bits,' I said, tripping over the words.

Mum's face crumpled with horror.

'Well, I want you to tell me a bit more. What do you mean?' She pushed for the gory details.

Now I was on the edge of tears. The dam holding the reservoir was about to break. I crumbled and said, 'He's been having sex with me.'

Mum burst into tears. She was crying so hard her whole body heaved up and down. I couldn't bear seeing her so sad. I started to cry because I felt so guilty. *You did this, Tina. Look what you've done.*

'Come 'ere,' Mum sobbed and put her arms around me. She had never really hugged me in all my fourteen years. The warmth spread across me like a blanket and I nestled into her chest.

'I'm really sorry. I'm really sorry,' she said, gently rocking me like I was a baby.

'You do believe me, don't you?' I cried.

'Yeah,' she hushed me.

'Mum, I'm not lying,' I whimpered.

'I know, I know,' she reassured me.

We sat there hugging for what felt like for ever. Our tears seeping together into her work blouse. I don't know what she was thinking but all I felt was deep, heart-wrenching guilt. I was convinced I was to blame and I was terrified what problems opening my big mouth were going to cause. *Was I going to be taken away by Social Services? Is Dave going to beat the crap out of me?* I was crying and shaking and I didn't want my mum to ever let me go.

12

The Ultimate Betrayal

I was terrified about what was going to happen next.

It was unnerving to see my mum so upset, and my life as I knew it turned upside down. There's nothing worse than feeling out of control. My mum couldn't offer me the reassurance I needed because she was too distraught. I was sent away into the darkness again.

'Go to your bedroom, he's going to be home in a minute,' she instructed, drying her eyes with her hands.

I nodded and scurried back to my room. I had lost all the protective armour I'd built around me over the years of abuse. I shut the door and clambered onto my bed just before my knees gave way. I tucked my legs into my chest just like I would have done in Mum's womb, and rocked back and forth.

The front door slammed. He was home.

I froze and listened hard to every footstep.

'Can you come here?' Mum yelled from her bedroom.

Oh, my God, Oh, my God.

'In a minute,' he grunted back.

'No, NOW!' she bellowed.

I lay as still as if I was dead. He trudged up the stairs and past my bedroom. Mum told him to shut her door behind him. I couldn't hear what was said but there was shouting and swearing and crying. I heard my mum sob like never before.

I lay there, hating myself. I wanted to punch my legs I felt so guilty. *It's all my fault. I've really upset Mum. Oh, my God, what is going to happen?* I felt sick with worry.

The shouting and crying went on and on and I was helpless to stop it. Eventually the bedroom door swung open.

I held my breath, my heart stopped, and my stomach reached out of my mouth. *What is going to happen now? I shook with fear. Are they going to come into my room? Please no.* The front door opened and shut and then Mum started crying again and I assumed he'd left.

I didn't know what to do – whether to come out of my bedroom or stay put. To say something or to disappear? It was ages before I heard anything.

'Tina, can you come back in 'ere,' Mum called. I peeled myself off my mattress and nervously walked back in to face the music. Mum hadn't moved, she was still slumped over on her bed. Her eyes were puffy and red and you could barely make out their blue colour for the enraged veins splintering through them.

I stood there, wobbling like a sail in a storm.

'He's gone,' she whispered. 'I've told him he's got to get out.' She looked up at me.

'OK,' I said. Still terrified.

She sighed with her whole body and then told me her plan. 'I'm going to tell Blake he's had an affair and we're just going to go from there . . .' Her voice started to crack again.

'OK.' I nodded, trying to hold on to my tears.

And that was it. Nothing else was said. There was no 'Let's ring the police.' I was dismissed like I'd been sent to the teacher for detention.

I went back to my bedroom and curled up in the same foetal position. I was frightened because I'd opened Pandora's box and I had no idea what was going to spring out next. I gently rocked myself like Mum had done to me earlier. A tiny smile danced across my face as I felt the first flicker of relief that Dave would not be raping me that night.

Hang on a minute, *Mum had said Dave had gone, but she didn't say he'd never be coming back. Where has he gone? To work? To the pub?* So many questions were whirring around my head but I was too frightened to ask Mum because she was already so upset I didn't want to make it worse for her.

I was crying in my room and she was crying in her room, and although there was only Blake's bedroom separating us, it felt like we could have been at separate ends of the world. I felt so lonely and all I wanted was for her to come into my room and hug me, and tell me she loved me, and that it was going to be OK. I may have had to grow up quickly but I was still a kid. A fourteen-year-old who just wanted her mum.

I have no memory of how time passed on the Saturday. I

can't remember waking up, or even doing our usual Saturday cleaning chores. What I do remember is the gentle feeling of relief seeping through me from my head to my toes as the day passed. By the evening I was starting to remember what happy feels like, or rather, what it actually feels like to be happy. Blake didn't even annoy me that night and for a moment I believed that we would carry on like a family, as if Dave never existed.

Sunday passed without Dave, and I was listening to some music in my room when Mum hollered up the stairs.

'Tina, can you come down?' she shouted.

It was the tone she always used when I was in trouble for something.

'In a minute,' I yelled back over my cassette player in my stroppy teenager voice.

'No, it's really important. Can you come down?' she shouted back.

I switched off my Wet Wet Wet music and reluctantly stomped downstairs into the living room. I was wearing my usual baggy jeans and T-shirt to hide my body. Mum was standing with one arm across her chest, the other nervously holding a cigarette.

'Sit there,' she said, pointing to the armchair that was part of our fake-leather three-piece suite. She was fidgety and nervous and I felt guilty again for making her feel like this.

She handed me a tumbler with ice and a dark liquid. One sniff and I knew it was Bacardi and Coke – Mum's favourite.

'Thanks,' I said hesitantly. I took a sip and it nearly blew my head off it was so strong.

'Do you want a cigarette? There are twenty fags there for ya,' she said, pointing to the box on the arm of the chair.

It was all very weird and alarm bells started to ring. I was only fourteen and she was offering me booze and fags. She looked jittery and uncomfortable and I didn't know how to handle her mood.

'I need to talk to you about Dave and what we are going to do,' she said, looking at the ground and then back at me nervously. She had perched herself at the edge of the sofa opposite.

'Have a drink,' she encouraged. I forced another glug down, burning my throat.

'Without Dave, we are going to really struggle financially,' she blurted. 'I don't really know how I'm going to manage to pay for all of us. We've just bought this house, so we have a mortgage to pay off.'

I stared at her blankly.

'Problem is, if I can't pay the mortgage and bills then we're going to end up on the streets,' she said calmly.

I didn't know where she was going with this. I was sitting there innocently, forcing back my Bacardi and Coke.

'You don't want to see your little brother Jonathan on the streets, do ya?' she asked, her eyes turning into marble.

The words speared my heart. I loved Jonathan like he was my own son. I'd made a promise to him that I would always protect him and I couldn't be the one responsible for making us homeless. Little did I know at the time but the council would never have let that happen or they would have forced Dave to pay the mortgage. I had to take my mum's word for it.

I watched in horror as Mum sucked a long inhale on her cigarette. She washed it down with her glass of Bacardi and Coke. The clinking ice cubes filled the awkward silence.

'But we have got an option,' she said.

'OK,' I said, cocking my head to the side sceptically.

'If he moves back in . . .' she started.

As soon as she said that, I threw my head back with fear and disgust.

'No, no, hear me out.' She tried to control the situation.

'O . . . K,' I said and listened.

'What if he moves back in, but for no other reason than for money.'

My jaw dropped to the floor.

'You'll be all right because we'll get a lock put on your bedroom door. And I will wear a key for our room around my neck and, if he needs to go to the toilet in the night, I'll let him out and then lock him back in.' She did her best sales pitch.

I just didn't know what to say.

'Listen, it's up to you. He doesn't have to come back here and I would understand why because what he has done is wrong,' she added.

I opened my mouth to speak and then. 'But if he doesn't come back we will all be on the streets . . .' came the guilt trip.

'But it's up to you, it is your decision.' She pretended to give me an option again.

What choice did I have? I never thought once about myself but I thought how could I possibly put my little brother on the street? How can I take away his home? I couldn't even do it to Blake. Or my mum, despite everything she had done for me. *After all, I am to blame for this.*

I took a deep breath and gave her what she wanted – him rather than me.

'OK, let him back in,' I whispered.

13

Lost the Will

If your own mother doesn't protect you, what hope is there?

In the blink of an eye she had managed to turn the spotlight off Dave and onto me, as the safety of my family was put on my shoulders. The sad thing is, I had become so desperate, that her choosing *him* over *me* only made me want to win her love even more. I was torn between hating her guts and hating myself so much, I reasoned why she would despise me too.

My life changed from that day – I finally knew for certain that I wouldn't be saved. There was to be no more daydreaming how my mum would come to my rescue. I just had to get on with surviving the best I could.

I got up for school on Monday morning like all the times before. I had breakfast in silence with Blake, while Mum rushed around getting ready for work. It was like nothing had happened. Mrs Walsh asked how it went and I told her Mum was going to put a lock on my door. She gave me her address, if ever I needed her help, and she handed me a whistle, which I was to blow if Dave came into my room again. That was it. There was no calling the police, no speaking to Social Services, no taking me away from my house of abuse – it was up to me to fend for myself. I was still in such shock from *him* being allowed back in that I barely remember my conversation with Mrs Walsh. But the memory of being let down, again, will stay with me for ever.

That whole day passed as a messy blur of nothingness. I stuck close to Sam's side. She couldn't believe my mum had let Dave back in.

'What are you going to do?' she said.

As far as I was concerned, it was already dead and buried.

'Nothing,' I shrugged.

'What?' Sam asked in disbelief.

I shrugged again.

'Tina?' Sam shrieked, trying to get through to me.

'I don't care any more. Forget it,' I dismissed her. 'Wanna go for a smoke?' I suggested, to take the heat off me.

Dave wasn't home when I got back from school, but I had a brand-spanking-new lock on my bedroom door. It was a round lock and the end of the key looked like a screwdriver. My mum was useless with DIY, so there was only one person who would have installed it – the same person it was designed to keep out.

I pulled open my drawer and rummaged for any key rings I'd collected. I attached one, and then another, then another, weighing down the key so, if Dave tried to push it out from the other side of the lock, I'd hear it crash to the ground. I had to do everything I could to stop him getting to me because I knew, if I felt his hands on me again, I would be too scared to fight him off.

I locked myself in my room but I didn't feel any safer. I couldn't put my trust in a flimsy lock – I couldn't put my trust in anyone or anything any more. I felt like a sitting duck because I didn't know if Dave would find another way to rape me. When I went downstairs later that evening, he was slouched on the sofa watching TV with Mum. His legs were sprawled apart and his fat belly rolled over his tracksuit bottoms. He looked up for a moment, our eyes caught, and then he dismissed me like I was nothing. There was no stare of death for telling on him, there was no awkwardness, it was like he'd never been kicked out of the house. It was like he had never raped me for all those years. Mum had her feet up and was engrossed by whatever was flashing across the screen.

I hate you. I hate you! I shouted through my eyes at her. Dave had only been back for a few hours but what he'd done to me had already been forgotten. *Am I worth so little?* Blake was in the kitchen rummaging for snacks and Jonathan was playing at Mum's feet, both oblivious to the drama of the weekend. I looked at them all and realised I didn't belong there any more.

I became a recluse, locked in my bedroom. I kept my door secured at all times and I only went downstairs for food and drink. I couldn't relax and dreaded taking a bath because Dave would always magically appear outside just at the moment I crossed the landing to my bedroom. I could feel his eyes boring a hole through the door at me. I felt exposed and vulnerable sitting naked in the bath water and it brought flashbacks to when Dave insisted on scrubbing between my legs when I was six years old.

I splashed the water over my legs and chest, hoping it would wash the past away, but the memory bombs kept dropping. Our bathroom was too poky to get dressed in so I had to walk across the landing in my towel. I chose the biggest one I could find in the airing cupboard but it still left some flesh for him to ogle at.

'Three, two, one, go' – I counted myself down. I opened the door to make my run, just like the gates opening at the dog racing.

I bashed into Dave, who was hovering outside.

'Sorry,' he mumbled, but I kept running, until I had my bedroom door locked behind me. I hated that he got to see some flesh, it made me want to wash myself again. I'd become a prisoner in my home.

I don't know if Mum noticed I'd become even more down or if she just needed to ease her conscience, but a couple of weeks later she brought up the past. We were sitting in the front room, and as usual there was no warm-up conversation, she blurted it out.

'Dave's going for counselling,' she stated. I was only fourteen, I had no idea what that meant. I looked at her blankly.

'Do you want to go?' she asked, forcing the corners of her mouth up into a smile.

'What is it?' I shrugged.

Mum explained it was a professional who I could talk to

about what Dave had done. That it might help me get over it.

'Well?' she said.

'Ummmm.' I mulled it over. I didn't want to talk to a stranger about something I'd had to keep a secret for so many years. *How would I even begin to tell someone about the things I'd never been able to share?* The thought was so uncomfortable it sent a shiver down my spine.

'OK, I'll do it,' I mumbled. I could tell she really wanted me to go and all I wanted to do was please her. I'd still do anything to win her love.

'Great, I think it will help you,' she said, and smiled.

The counsellor had a clinic in a house in Romford, and Mum drove me there after school. I didn't have any idea what to expect – I imagined a woman with big glasses dressed in a white coat. *Would I be put into a straitjacket like they do in the movies? What will she ask me? Will she examine me?* I had so many questions but I sat through that car journey in silence. I was too afraid to ask Mum. I'd opened up to her about what Dave had been doing to me, we'd hugged and cried together, but we were now back to being barely civil.

'It's going to help,' she said as we pulled up. I think she was reassuring herself rather than me.

A tiny woman with petite features shook my nervous hand and led me into her office. The blinds were shut and there was a warm glow coming from a lamp in the corner. Her chair was next to what looked like a cross between a hospital bed and a sofa. She signalled me to take a seat on the bed.

'Just lie back and try to relax,' she said in a sickly sweet voice.

I didn't want to lie back in a dark room, it made me feel vulnerable. It was like being back in my bedroom moments before Dave raped me. I waited for her to settle back in the grooves of her chair, which she'd moulded over the years of speaking to patients.

'It's OK, lie back,' she reassured me. I slowly lowered myself, my body rigid, just like when Dave used to touch me in my bed.

'So, Tina . . .' She brought her fingertips together. 'I just want to find out a little bit more about you,' she said, and smiled.

I don't like you. I felt like I didn't belong there, although I had no idea where I did belong any more. I listened to her questions for Mum's sake so at least I could tell her I tried. She broke the ice by asking me about my childhood, skirting around what I was really there for. I folded my arms across my chest, I could tell she was trying to build a rapport but I didn't want to be her friend.

'Tina?' she said. I'd drifted off into another world while she was talking to me.

'It's very important we trust each other,' she carried on. 'You can trust me.' She smiled.

I wanted to believe her but everyone I'd put my trust in had let me down. I told myself to relax and give her a chance.

'You don't have to worry, nothing you tell me will I share with David,' she announced.

What? You're counselling my stepdad as well? I couldn't believe that Mum had sent us to the same person. Another kick in the teeth. Another person who has betrayed me.

'How do I know you won't tell him stuff I've told you?' I snapped.

'I won't; what you tell me is confidential.' She tried to calm me down.

I knotted my arms even tighter across my chest. She carried on trying to reassure me but there was now a brick wall between us. There was no way I was going to tell this lady anything because it could get back to Dave. The things in my head were the only part of my body my stepdad hadn't abused, the one thing that belonged to me that he couldn't take away. I felt that if I opened up to this stranger then he would still be able to get to me.

'OK, Tina, we've run out of time for this week but next week we'll talk a little more in depth about what's happened,' she said, smiling, then ushering me out the door. *Thank God we've run out of time*, I thought as I threw her a sarcastic smile. Mum was waiting in the car outside.

'How did it go?' she asked.

'Uh, OK I guess,' I lied, as we battled through the rush-hour traffic.

That elephant was back on my chest and I was straining to breathe. Was there anyone I could trust? I'd felt angry while I was in that room but now I felt incredibly sad and lonely. It was dark so Mum couldn't see the tears trickling down my cheeks.

'I don't want to go and see her any more,' I said.

'What? Are you sure?'

'Yep,' I insisted.

'Oh, OK.' She shrugged.

And that was the end of it. We never talked about the abuse again while I lived at home. It became the elephant in the room that everyone pretended not to see. I didn't have my mum, I didn't have my brothers, I didn't have my teachers. I had no one to protect me. I'd lock myself in my bedroom and play music and cry. Punching my body became the only way to feel calm as sometimes I felt so unhappy, so lonely, I wanted to die.

I lost all interest in school in my final year. I couldn't give a damn what grades I got. I bunked off most lessons to smoke down the park with my friends or hang around in the town centre. When I was at school I walked around like I owned the place and did everything to break the rules. I'd have my blouse hanging out and I was always getting detention for wearing too much make-up – I caked my face in orange foundation and blue eyeshadow to hide the real me.

The teachers complained to my mum about my behaviour but she didn't seem to care. After she let Dave back in, I could get away with murder. My 8.30 p.m. curfew went out the window, I was no longer tied to the kitchen sink, I could do whatever I wanted.

But the freedom I once craved wasn't so appealing now it was handed on a plate. The food she was serving up was her guilt, and it tasted off. Having Mum shouting was better than being ignored, because at least she noticed me when she was hitting me. I felt even lonelier, even more unloved, even more worthless. I did everything I could to get out of the house – I'd stay out late drinking in the park or spend the night around friends' houses. By the time I was doing my final exams at school I was at home only two nights a week. I even tried to find a boyfriend so I'd be able to have somewhere to stay and someone to pay me attention.

Robbie was three years older than me and he used to hang around the park with his mates. We'd stayed friends since I met him at the arcades on my last holiday to Highfields. He was a fabrication welder and lived over the bridge in Swanscombe, Kent. Robbie was tall and skinny with black hair that parted in the middle like curtains, and the girls thought he wasn't bad-looking. I was desperate for attention so I'd put on my Tough Tina act to try to win his heart. I hated my body and my hair and my curves so I played the tomboy who clowned around with the lads. I tried to keep up with their drinking and smoking and we were knocking back the cider on the park bench when he leant in and kissed me for the first time.

My heart said one thing but my body did another – I froze just like when Dave smothered me with his mouth. He pulled away a little but was still close enough for me to feel his breath on my face.

'Relax,' he teased, shaking his curtains out of his long dark eyelashes.

How could I relax? I wanted him to like me so badly but I felt horrible when he touched my skin. I threw on my bravado so he didn't think I was a silly little schoolgirl.

'Give me some of that,' I said, snatching the two-litre

cider bottle from his hand, tipping it down my throat. I puckered my lips and leant forward so he could meet me halfway. His mouth touched mine and I hated the wetness of his tongue. How was I supposed to breathe? Where was I supposed to put my hands? My fingers were clenched around the bench seat as I let him do what he wanted with me. If that's what it takes for someone to like me then I was prepared to do anything. When he finished, Robbie threw his arm around me and that was the part that felt nice. Feeling the warmth of his cuddle brought me back to life and I sank into his shoulder and closed my eyes and imagined I didn't ever have to go back home.

I was so desperate not to lose him that I was willing to give Robbie anything he wanted. Through Dave, I'd learnt that sex was the way to get attention, to get someone to be nice to me. So when Robbie pushed for it, I let him take me. We'd only been dating a few weeks and we were watching TV on his sofa while his parents were upstairs in bed. His lounge was a big L shape that sprouted from the bottom of the staircase, putting us in full view if his parents were to come down but I didn't care about being caught. What was there to be afraid of once you've been raped by your step-dad?

Robbie had a way of cupping my face in his big workman's hands when he kissed me, just like they did in the movies.

'You're really pretty,' he whispered in my ear as he nuzzled at my neck. I felt an explosion in my heart at those magic words.

'No, I'm not,' I said, flirting through my eyelashes. I

wanted him to keep paying me compliments. He pushed his weight onto me, *just like Dave did*, forcing me down onto my back on the sofa. I saw that flash of hunger in his eyes and his breath got heavy, *just like Dave's did*. My eyes automatically closed but I prized them open – I didn't want this to be like all the other times. Robbie fumbled with his belt and unzipped his flies and I did the same with my jeans. It was rushed and messy and I didn't really know what was happening. Most girls would have wanted their first time to be in a bedroom, or somewhere romantic, but I didn't care. Most girls would have been afraid about their first time, especially at fourteen years old, but I didn't have anything to fear – I'd had sex hundreds of times already.

I wriggled my pants to my ankles and he pushed his boxer shorts over his bum and he pressed against me, *just like Dave did*, and again, and then he pushed into me. I forced my eyes open because I wanted to see him, I wanted it to feel real. I wished more than anything that Robbie was the one to take my virginity. It was over in seconds and I didn't feel anything. Where were the fireworks everyone talks about? My body was an empty vessel that had turned numb years ago.

We quickly put our jeans back on and Robbie gave me a lingering kiss. He pulled me back into a cuddle and we carried on watching TV like two naughty teenagers. The wave of excitement quickly passed and I was left with a hollow ache in my stomach. I wanted to be loved and be needed, so badly, but the dirty stain of the past was tattooed all over my skin. I could never have a normal relationship with Robbie because my stepdad had taken me first.

'Ha, ha, let's watch this,' Robbie laughed, switching over to a comedy sketch, oblivious to the tears that were trickling down my cheeks.

'Yeah, this looks good,' I joined in. I didn't care what we watched, as long as his arm stayed locked around me like an anchor, stopping me from drifting off into my dark past.

'I love you,' I mumbled.

'Errr . . .' He squirmed. 'I love you too,' he said, embarrassed.

We were only young but those words meant more to me than he could ever know. *Maybe I wasn't so worthless after all?*

I couldn't wait to tell Mum and Dave I had a boyfriend because I was certain it would turn their heads. I should have known better – Mum was just grateful that someone, anyone, had taken me off her hands. She didn't even have to go through the safe-sex chat with me because I was already on the pill to ease my period pains. Dave didn't say a word, he just glared at Robbie from his chair in the lounge if Robbie ever came to mine to pick me up. What could Dave say? He had a lot to be grateful for – he'd got away with raping me for four years.

I stayed most of the week in Robbie's parents' spare room, conjuring up a plan to take me far away from my family. I'd imagine what it would be like if I became an orphan – if Mum was killed in a car crash and everyone was begging me to come to her funeral, only for me to turn around and say no, to spite her. Some days I hated her so much for choosing *him* over me, I wished her dead. As long as she was alive I'd never feel I was good enough.

I finished secondary school with D and E grades and took a job as a trainee hairdresser in a salon in Barking so I could earn enough money to leave home. I had no drive, no ambition; I couldn't care less what I did with my life as long as I got away from my abuser. When I turned seventeen I'd built up enough experience to start a mobile hairdressing business. I could finally afford to escape, so I moved in with Robbie. Our studio flat in Gravesend was going to be the fresh start I'd always dreamt of – a new home where we could make new memories, where I could leave the past behind.

PART TWO

14

No Escape

My head felt like someone had put an axe through it.
I leant it against the window of the bus as it took me home to Romford after another Saturday night partying in Crystal Palace. The old woman across the aisle glared at me disapprovingly, as I was still wearing my clothes from the night before. I couldn't have looked more out of place with my sparkling sequin top and gold stilettos and mascara smudged down my face.

I smelt of the night before as well. *I smelt of him.* Whoever 'he' was – I hadn't caught his name before I'd snuck out of his bedroom at 8 a.m., my eleventh one-night stand in three months. I closed my eyes from the throbbing hangover and a flashback sent me spinning.

Me, half-naked, on the living-room floor, having sex with a guy who I'd met at the bar three hours earlier. I squirmed in my seat from the embarrassing memory. I closed my eyes again. Another flashback, this time the smell of Old Spice. My conquest wore my stepdad's favourite aftershave. I retched, and I thought I was going to be sick.

I held my fist to my mouth as if that would stop the

vomit. The old lady looked at me in horror and I glared back, as if to say, 'Mind your own business.' Not only did I feel sick as a dog, I felt dirty and cheap and all I wanted to do was scrub my skin clean of him. *Why did you have sex with him when you know it makes you feel this way?* I scolded myself. I knew why, because I craved attention, because I was lonely, because I thought if I slept with them, they would love me.

Since Robbie had left to take a job in Wolverhampton, my life had spiralled out of control. We'd tried to stay together but the distance had left me feeling very lonely, the feeling I dreaded most in the world. I took a Saturday job, singing karaoke at a bar in Crystal Palace during the summer of 1992, when I was seventeen, and moved to a bedsit in Romford, to save money while Robbie was away. The attention I got from singing on stage was just like the dreams I used to have as a kid and I couldn't say no when the men asked me back to theirs. The feeling of the morning after was lonelier than the night before. I wanted the earth to swallow me up as I made the endless bus journey back to my flat where I would be spending more time alone. My tears smudged on the windowpane as we bounced over the speed bumps into my estate. I bit my lip to stop myself sobbing – that would be the final humiliation.

I wobbled through the door in my tired stilettos and stumbled into the bathroom, leaving the door open behind me. I never shut doors now because it reminded me of Dave trapping me in my bedroom. I climbed into the shower and stood there like a statue, letting the water wash off the grime like rain. My skin was wrinkly by the time I got out and I wrapped myself in a big fluffy towel and dived under my duvet. I was exhausted but I couldn't sleep, I needed to do something first, something I hadn't done in a while. I sat up and raised my fists and hammered down on my legs.

I was going through a dark time in my life, where most girls would have called on their mum for help, but she wasn't someone to go to when I was in trouble. We still spoke on the phone now and again and I'd sometimes visit her when my washing machine was on the blink, but I kept my worries to myself, just like I'd done for all those years when Dave had abused me.

I didn't even tell her when I fell pregnant at eighteen with a guy I'd been seeing for only a couple of months. It was an accident and we broke up shortly after I found out, but I'd rather talk to a virtual stranger than her.

'My boyfriend's bringing a mate round my house tonight for a DVD,' said Debbie, one of my hairdressing clients – practically a stranger.

The thought of being sociable was the last thing on my mind. I was eighteen, ten weeks pregnant with a guy I barely knew, living alone in a grotty flat, with no one to turn to for help.

'Come, it'll be a laugh.' She coaxed me into it.

Her boyfriend's friend turned out to be the crutch I desperately needed to lean on. I sat next to John on the sofa and stayed there chatting until 8 a.m., when he had to prise himself up to go to work. He was twenty-six and a bit of a bad boy with tattoos over his arms, shoulder-length curly hair, six foot, broad shoulders and liked to brag about the fights he'd been in. I was drawn to him because he made me feel safe, like he would protect me from harm with his muscles.

He was a plumbing and central-heating engineer and he came to see me after he finished work that same day – and never left. He told me he wanted to look after me and my baby and a month later I was meeting his parents. He was like a plaster covering my wounds and I believed he would be the one to finally help me forget my past. I didn't tell him much about me. I vowed a long time ago I would never tell a soul what my stepdad had done – if I didn't talk about it, I could pretend it never happened. I was sure I would lose him if he knew how dirty I really was.

We were at his mum's house having tea and biscuits, sheltering from the biting cold outside, when I felt a sharp pain in my womb. It was December 1993. I was three and a half months pregnant and hadn't had any problems up until now. I leant forward, clutching my stomach as another wave of pain hit me.

'*Uggghh*,' I grimaced. I felt like I was going to be sick.

'You should go to hospital,' John's mum insisted. She was a nurse. I told them to stop making a fuss – my pain threshold was incredibly high thanks to all those years of being raped – but John dragged me into the car and took me to Rush Green A&E.

I was rushed into theatre with a suspected ectopic pregnancy. I came around from the anaesthetic to a burning pain in my lower back. I looked down to find a huge cut across my belly. I was then told the bad news – I'd lost the baby and one of my Fallopian tubes.

It's always the same with life – you never know how much you want something, or someone, until you lose them. I didn't realise quite how much I wanted a baby until it was snatched from me. More than anything I wanted to be loved, and I realised having a child was the only way to get that sort of unconditional love. I wanted to have a baby so I could love them and look after them and put them first. I wanted to be the mum I'd always longed for.

'Hi, babe.' John was finally allowed to see me. My eyes were red and puffy from crying.

He pulled up a plastic chair next to my bed and took my hand gently in his.

'I've brought you something.' He smiled, bringing a box of Maltesers from behind his back.

I laughed through my tears.

'I think we should get married. I love ya,' he said.

Those words tipped me over the edge and I broke down in sobs.

'Hey, hey, that was supposed to make you happy,' he joked, wiping the tears from my face with his rough hands.

'I am happy,' I blubbed. 'Yes, I will marry you,' I said and kissed him.

I'd only known John weeks, but I thought I loved him. I needed someone to protect me and I loved being loved by him. I pulled his face close to mine and kissed him again. He stroked my hand for what felt like for ever and then broke the news he had to leave me. He was off to a Wet Wet Wet concert I should have been going to.

'I hate you,' I said, and thumped my fists on the bed. They were my favourite band, who I'd listened to for hours at a time in my bedroom when I was a kid.

'I'll bring you back a T-shirt,' he teased.

'Go on, get out of here,' I sniffed.

I was in a ward with three empty beds, and that desperate feeling of being alone crept up on me after John left. I tried to fight off the next storm of tears, but when the lights went out and I was trapped in the dark with only the foreign noises of a hospital as comfort – I broke down.

All I wanted to do was curl up in a ball like I used to do when I was a kid, but I was in too much pain to move. I stopped missing John and started missing my mum. I was that little girl again who needed a hug from her mum. I needed her to wrap her arms around me and tell me it was going to be OK. I hated her for not being there for me.

Back home, my way of dealing with the loss of my baby was the same way I dealt with everything – block out the pain.

'Do you want to try some acid?' John offered me a small square of paper he'd bought off our neighbour.

I stared at the drug for a moment. I'd just recovered from a major operation, what was I thinking?

'Yeah, why not?' I smiled, holding out my hand. I wasn't scared, I had nothing to lose. I put the paper in my mouth and let it melt on my tongue.

'Nothing's happening,' I complained to John who was chatting to some mates he'd invited over.

'Just wait,' he said, and grinned.

Half an hour later we were all in hysterics, to the point I could barely breathe. I couldn't remember the last time I'd laughed so hard and I couldn't stop. That night was the first of many drug-infused weekends at our flat. It masked the pain that was eating me from inside. It helped me forget about my baby, about the horrific rape flashbacks, about my mum who should have protected me. But I quickly learnt the problem with getting high, was coming down the next day. It brought my pain to the surface, it released my anger and I took it out on the closest person to me – John.

I sat on our bed, trembling, after another sleepless night. I scratched the skin on my arms and legs to try to calm myself down, crying out for help.

'You don't love me!' I screamed, as he tried to get ready for work.

'Why are you with me?' I provoked. I needed his attention.

'I don't have time for this shit,' he said, as he walked off into the living room. The fire ignited in the pit of my stomach. The anger I'd held inside for so many years rose to the surface like a volcano. The frustration at not having the guts to tell John about my dark secret.

'Don't walk out of this room!' I yelled as he reached for the front door. The monster inside ripped out of my skin and picked up the eight-inch glass ashtray on the coffee table. I was that angry girl again, who used to scrap in the playground. I hurled the ashtray at his head.

SMASH! It splintered into a million pieces against the wall, missing John's face by millimetres.

'What the fuck?' he yelled, cowering under his hands.

I was shaking from the realisation of what I'd just done. John had a temper too and I could see the fire in his eyes.

'You're fucking nuts.' He waved his arms. I thought he was going to go for me but he managed to pull himself out of the fire and stormed out. I collapsed onto the floor, crying. *What did you do that for, Tina? No wonder no one loves you.*

I hit myself.

We brushed over our differences by getting off our heads on drugs. We were having one of our party weekends when our washing machine broke down, again. My dirty laundry was one of the only reasons I still kept in contact with Mum.

I rang her before she headed off to work. It was Monday, the end of February 1994.

'Pop over and use our machine,' Mum said. She hung up just before I had a chance to ask whether Dave would be at home. I grabbed an armful of whites and asked John if he could drop me off at my old house in Rush Green.

I shivered every time I walked up the drive. It was a house full of ghosts but I had to grin and bear it if I was to get our washing done. I knocked on the door.

Please don't be in, please don't be in. I prayed Dave was at work.

No answer.

The coast was clear so I unlocked the door and let myself into the living room. The smell of stale chip fat hung in the air and I could see the ghost of Blake and me fighting over the TV controls. I tossed my clothes in the washing machine and collapsed on the sofa, hoping to get a little snooze while I waited for the cycle to finish.

I quickly sailed into a deep sleep. I don't know how long I was out for but I was woken to something tugging at the button on my jeans. I slowly rolled up my eyelids, waiting for the sleep haze to clear.

Another tug and then another.

What the . . . ? I looked up to see my stepdad standing over me – naked.

His trousers and pants were around his ankles and he'd placed his penis in my hand, which was hanging off the sofa. He was grinning like a cat that had got the cream.

I froze with fear just like I had done for all those years he had abused me. *What do I do?* My heart hammered in my ears but the adrenalin wasn't making me run. *Why can't I run away?*

Run, RUN.

This time I didn't shut my eyes and pretend I was dead. I was eighteen years old, not a defenceless ten-year-old. *I am not going to let this happen again!* the fighter in me screamed.

'Get off!' I shouted, shaking my hand free and pushing him out of my way. I couldn't bear to look at his lecherous face as I bundled my washing into the basket. Luckily he had made himself scarce by the time I ran for the door. I ran down the drive, along the street. I didn't stop running until my exhausted legs couldn't physically carry me any further.

I don't remember how I got back to Romford, I was in such a state. My make-up from the weekend had smudged down my face, thanks to the rivers of tears.

'Come on, COME ON!' I screamed at the keys, as I tried to wriggle them into the lock on my flat.

'Noooo,' I sobbed, as my shaky hands dropped them on the pavement.

I fell through the door and slammed it shut with my back. The room was hot and spinning. I stumbled forwards, my arms flaying for something to grab hold of. I propped myself up on the kitchen work surface and then yanked opened the cupboards. I thrashed through them, looking for something to finally end my torture. I scooped up every pill pot from paracetamol to aspirins and grabbed a bottle of vodka to wash the lethal cocktail down.

I stumbled through my blizzard of tears to the bathroom and spilled the hundreds of pills across the top of our washing machine. My knees gave way and I crashed to the floor, hugging the vodka. I was howling from the pain I felt inside. I didn't want to go on any more. I realised no matter what I did I'd never be able to get away from my stepdad.

I reached up and grabbed a handful of pills.

15

Trying to Forget

'Tina?'

One of my friends must have heard me sobbing.

'*Tina?*' Sarah, an old school friend, screeched. I'd left the front door unlocked and she had let herself in, hoping to catch me for a cup of tea. Sarah got a lot more than she bargained for, as she found me curled up in a ball on the bathroom floor.

I was shaking and sobbing, snot was running down my face and my hair was glued across my cheeks.

'What's happened?' She panicked, shaking my shoulders.

'Leave me alone,' I howled.

'What's gone on?' she shouted, terrified by the sea of pills scattered around me.

I just couldn't tell her. I couldn't tell anyone, I was so ashamed.

'Just leave me alone!' I screamed, pushing her away with my hands.

She tackled me to the ground. 'I can't leave you like this. What the fuck has happened?'

There was a knock on the door. It was my chance to push

Sarah away, because as long as she was in the bathroom with me, I wouldn't be able to kill myself.

'Get that,' I ordered. She ran to see if it was John and I quickly reached up and turned the lock. No one could stop me now. I scooped up half-a-dozen more pills and tipped them into my mouth, washing them down with the bitter vodka.

'*Ahhhhaha*,' I coughed, buckling onto all fours. I took another swig of the bottle; the cheap alcohol burnt my throat. I'd decided I had nothing else to live for. It had been four years since he'd violated me like that. He hadn't raped me but he might as well have done because it brought everything back.

'Open the door, open the door!' Sarah shouted from the other side of the door.

'Leave me alone,' I begged.

I heard John's gruff voice and my heart sank. Why did he have to come home from work early today? I knew he would stop me now.

'I don't know what the fuck's the matter with her but she's locked herself in the bathroom,' I heard Sarah screaming at John.

'Open the fucking door!' John yelled, banging with his fists.

'BANG!' he started kicking the door in.

I curled up into a ball again, shaking, sobbing.

'Just let me die,' I whispered.

BANG! BANG! BANG!

John broke the door down and charged in like a rhino, scooping me up into his big muscly arms.

'What's gone on?' he yelled at me.

I shook my head violently from side to side.

'Fucking tell me?' he shouted inches from my face. 'Who's hurt ya?' he kept going.

He didn't have a clue. I hadn't told a soul since I was fourteen, and the words were now trapped in my throat. He wrapped his big strong hands around my face and forced me to look him in the eye.

'Who's hurt ya?' he said again.

My lower lip trembled as the tears gushed from my eyes. I took a deep breath and told John what had happened:

'When you dropped me around Mum's this morning, my stepdad tried to make me touch him.' I took a deep breath.

'He tried to undress me,' I spluttered through my sobs.

'I can't deal with it. I want to die,' I howled, burying my head in his broad chest. It was the lowest I'd felt in my whole life.

I felt John's chest and arm muscles clench with anger. A river of red ran from his neck through his face.

'Fucking cunt!' he shouted, punching the door with his fist. 'I'm going to kill him, I'm going to fucking kill him,' he cried. Steam was coming out of his ears. I'd never seen him look so angry. He swept the pills off the washing machine into his pocket.

'No, John, leave it!' I cried. I wanted to forget it ever happened. John didn't listen; he was a bull in a china shop. He pointed his finger at Sarah.

'Make sure she doesn't take any more pills,' he ordered, and then stormed out the door. I heard the car screech as he drove off, and I panicked. John was a big guy and I was scared what he might do. I didn't want him to get in trouble with the police because of me. Sarah managed to move me from the cold bathroom floor to the sofa and I lay there in silence, gently rocking to calm my thoughts. It seemed like hours had passed before John finally came back. I jumped to attention, desperate to find out what harm he'd caused.

'What did you do?' I gasped.

John's eyes were still wild like an animal that'd been out hunting for meat. He paced the room, spitting with anger.

'We had an argument on their doorstep,' he said, playing it down.

'Come on, what did you do?' I pressed him for answers.

'I told your mum that he tried to rape you!' he shouted. 'Dave stood behind her on the doorstep the whole time like the fucking gutless bastard that he is.'

'What did you say to him?' I shook my head in disbelief.

'I told him he was a piece of shit, and if I ever see him walking up the street he'd better cross the road because I was gonna kill him.' John punched the air.

What John had done should have made me feel better but I was feeling so groggy from the drugs I'd taken. I felt like I was just hanging on by a thread and I didn't care what was happening.

'We're going to the police,' he insisted.

I shook my head stubbornly. 'I can't,' I said. I was sure they wouldn't believe me, because in my heart I believed the abuse was my fault. I'd accepted the money, those gifts.

'What do you mean, you can't? He's just attacked you.' He looked at me in disbelief.

He didn't know the half of it. I wasn't strong enough to go through with telling the police. I thought they would rip me to shreds and tell me it was my fault. I started rocking again and John sat next to me on the armrest. He looked incredibly sad. Tears welled in his eyes, he put his arm around me and we cried together.

I refused to speak to my mum for six months. I even missed her fortieth birthday in April because I was so angry with her. She'd protected him again. I just couldn't get my head around how a mother could do that to her daughter.

I got a job working evenings behind the bar at a local pub but I'd spend my days lying in bed, crying, churning over my childhood memories. My heart would ping pong between despising my mum and despising myself. I couldn't stop hurting so I got high on drugs to forget the pain.

I was on my own when the letter arrived. I instantly knew who had written it, as there was no mistaking that swirly handwriting. It was from Mum. *What did she want? What could she possibly have to say to me?* I put the letter down on the coffee table and stared at it, debating whether to open it or chuck it in the bin. I reached forward and then snapped my hands back as if it had bitten me. I cradled my hands in my lap for a moment and then swooped for it again – I had to know.

I tore the envelope open and pulled out a couple of sheets of paper that were filled with writing. Mum obviously had a lot she wanted to say to me. I started reading and my face dropped.

It was one long apology.

Tears welled in my eyes as she told me how sorry she was for taking Dave back after I told her how he had raped me. My lower lip trembled and my hands shook, as I read the words I'd been waiting to hear for five years.

'I hope you can forgive me,' she said.

The tears rained onto the paper, making ink puddles of her words. I was happy and sad at the same time.

As I read on, the anger kicked in, as Mum explained the reason she took Dave back was because she didn't want to be on her own, that she felt lonely without him.

'You don't know the meaning of the word lonely!' I screamed.

I couldn't believe she was telling me she had chosen a paedophile, who raped her only daughter, because she didn't want to be lonely. I'd been lonely my whole life and I still was lonely.

'You selfish bitch,' I choked, screwing up the paper in my fist. I sank my head into my hands and sobbed.

John found me in the same crumpled position hours later when he got in from work. I was staring into space like I'd had a lobotomy.

'What's happened?' John asked urgently. My attempted overdose was still raw in his memory.

'Are you hurt? What's wrong?' He dropped to my side.

I thrust the letter into his hand and let him read it for himself. I'd told John the skeleton of what Dave had done to me as a child but he didn't know the half of it. I watched his eyes widen like saucers as he read my mum's plea for forgiveness. He shook his head in disgust and handed me back the letter.

'What are you going to do?' he barked. He was angry because he could see how upset I was.

'I really don't know,' I whispered, still staring into nothingness.

'Well, you're not going to forgive her, are ya?' John looked at me like I was mad.

'Are ya?' he badgered.

I shrugged. I didn't know what to do. My whole life, all I had wanted was for my mum to love me. I couldn't stop giving my mum one final chance to show me.

'I don't think you should have anything to do with her,' John said, flinging his arms in the air out of frustration. 'Look at what she did to you. She chose that pervert over you.'

'I know, but I have to forgive her, because she's my mum,' I cried. 'You only get one mum.'

John shook his head in bewilderment.

'Well, it's your decision.' He shrugged.

'I'm going to call her,' I announced.

John shrugged again.

'You're making a mistake,' he muttered, handing me the house phone.

My hands were shaking as I dialled Mum's number. John grabbed my hand and held it tightly to show his love and support. My heart was in my mouth as I waited for her to pick up.

''Ello,' came her familiar bark.

'Mum, it's Tina,' I said.

Silence.

'Well, say something,' I pushed.

I could hear her crying.

'I'm sorry,' she blubbered. 'I couldn't be without him,' she heaved between the tears.

I bit my lip in anger. I really wanted her to know what she had done to me, because ignoring my desperate plea for help when I was fourteen was almost worse than what Dave had done to me.

'Do you have any idea how lonely I've been?' I started. 'Do you?' My voice trembled from the painful memories.

'I can never get back my childhood. I can never get back my virginity.' My whole body was now shaking with sadness.

'The only thing I get to keep for ever –' I could barely get the words out '– is the memory of what *he* has done to me.'

I broke down sobbing.

Mum was crying too and, although there were miles between us, I finally felt her next to me, just like the time I sat on her bed and she wrapped her arms around me.

Mum told me she wanted to fix things, and I hung up, giving her yet another chance. I fell into John's chest, drained with emotion. He didn't speak but kissed my forehead as if to say he was there for me, whatever choice I made.

Mum and I spoke a couple of times a week over the phone and, with John by my side, the candle of hope reignited in my heart. Maybe I needed to go through all this pain to find happiness? So when I found I was pregnant again, in July, I was over the moon.

'We're going to be a family!' I squealed, showing John the pregnancy test.

'What?' He shook his head in disbelief. 'I thought you were on the pill?'

'I am. I must be that one per cent that falls pregnant while using it.' I shook my head in amazement.

'It's bloody brilliant news,' John said, and hugged and kissed me. John had always talked about wanting to be a dad and, although I was only nineteen, I knew I was ready to be a mum. I stroked my tummy like there was already a bump showing.

'I'm going to be a mum.' I beamed. 'I'm going to the best mum. I'm never going to let anyone hurt you,' I said to the baby growing inside me.

Most of all, I couldn't wait to feel the love a mother shares with their child, the love I was robbed of.

16

New Life

'Push, Tina,' the midwife shouted in my ear.

'Arrrrrgh!' I screamed, as the contraction tore through me.

I vomited over myself.

'Have the epidural!' John shouted.

'No,' I said, shaking my head. I wanted to be as brave for as long as I could. It was second nature for me to put up with pain.

'Have the bloody epidural,' he insisted.

'*Arrrrrgh!*' I squeezed John's hand so hard I could have broken it. I was sick again.

'OK, OK, help me,' I relented. I couldn't stop the tears it hurt so much.

The nurse injected my spine and the pain eased immediately.

'Push,' the midwife ordered again.

'I can see the head, push,' she said.

'*Arrrgh!*' I screamed the hospital down.

Three more pushes and Mitchell was born at 2.45 p.m. on Saturday, 14 January 1995. John winced as he cut the umbilical cord and he was handed into my arms.

He was tiny, weighing only 5lbs and 11 ounces. I cradled him and his warmth spread through me like a hot-water bottle. He had the blondest hair and the bluest eyes – he was beautiful.

I kissed his button nose and my heart melted as he curled his tiny hand around my little finger. I couldn't believe I had made him. It was an indescribable feeling. None of the drugs I'd taken the year before could replace the rush of giving birth – it was the best buzz I'd had in my life.

'So you got what you wished for.' I smiled at John, who had wanted a son.

'He looks like ya,' John grinned, tears welling in his eyes.

'You big softie,' I teased.

With John cooing by my side, I felt like I was in a family for the first time in my life. I was so happy, so full of hope for the future. I leant forward and kissed Mitchell's little nose again.

'I will do everything in my power to protect you. Nothing will ever hurt you,' I whispered. He was my baby and I was going to give him the world.

Mum visited me in hospital and brought my little brother Jonathan along. She held Mitchell and told me he was beautiful. *She's proud of me, I've finally done something to impress her.*

'I think he's got your eyes,' I lied. I wanted to show my gratitude for her being nice to me. It was the closest we had ever been and I was determined to hang on to that feeling.

'We can go for walks in the park together,' I suggested, glowing with the thought of sharing motherhood with my mum.

'Yeah.' She nodded. Her eyes were already glazing over.

'And you can help me choose baby clothes,' I kept trying.

'Yeah,' she said.

It was just the way Mum was. I shrugged it off. What was important was that she was by my side, trying to make up for the harm she'd caused. I couldn't wait to leave hospital and have Mitchell all to myself. Life was really good for a while and I loved being a mum – I loved being needed and loved by my little one.

John helped with the night feeds but, after a couple of months, exhaustion set in. It hit me like a train out of nowhere and I struggled to get back on my feet. Mitchell had terrible colic and it would take me an hour and a half to wind him. No sooner had my head hit the pillow than I had to be up again to feed him, and I became delirious from lack of sleep. I'd burst into tears over the smallest things like a plate breaking or burning the rice for dinner. The problem was that I'd gone from being raped, to finally getting my life a bit sorted, to being attacked again, to trying to kill myself, to taking drugs and then becoming a mum, all in a short space of time – and I couldn't cope.

Unfortunately for John, being the closest to me, he got the brunt of my frustration. My tears turned into temper tantrums and I started throwing things at him when we argued. Plates, ashtrays, anything I could grab hold of. I should have done javelin for England with the speed I hurled our crockery across the living room.

He did his best to stay calm but like anything you push too hard – it finally snaps. It is never OK for a man to hit a woman but I was horrible to John. He finally bit back after I'd suffered another long sleepless night.

Please bring up some air, please. Tears ran down my cheeks as I gently rubbed Mitchell's back.

'I love you, bubba, but please burp for Mummy,' I cried.

I could hear John snoring next door and I despised him for having a good night's sleep.

I hate you. I hate you. I hate you.

I kissed Mitchell and my tears dribbled onto his cheeks. I felt out of control. I eventually fell asleep on the sofa, watching *Prisoner: Cell Block H*.

'*Waaaaaaaa . . .*' I was jolted awake by Mitchell screaming.

'*Waaaaaaaa,*' he wailed.

'I'm coming, Mummy's coming.' I groaned, peeling myself off the sofa. I walked past our bedroom to find John still asleep.

'John, wake up, you're late for work,' I snapped.

He rolled over and the angry monster inside me reared its ugly head.

'Get up, John,' I snarled. I hated the fact that he was having a lie-in while I was yet again seeing to Mitchell.

He put the pillow over his head to block out the noise and I flipped.

'Get up!' I shouted in his ear.

SPLASH. I tipped a glass of cold water over him.

'You fucking bitch!' he yelled, jumping to his feet. John went for me and I ran for the front door, screaming.

'Help!' I shrieked as I yanked the door open.

I was no match for John though. He pinned me up against the wall in the hallway, using his forearm as a garrotte.

'Help!' I tried to scream but there was no air in my lungs.

John wrapped his hands around my neck and started squeezing. The room started to spin and I was seconds away from passing out. I thrashed my legs around, smashing a pile of milk bottles.

My face must have been blue by the time John let go. I fell to the ground like a sack of potatoes and he left me there, crying.

'*Waaaaaaaa*,' Mitchell screamed.

'Mummy's coming,' I whispered. I dried my tears like I'd done so many times before and got on with it.

John kept his distance after that and I spent many a night alone while he was down the pub with his friends. I envied the freedom he had to get up and leave and although my mum would pop in and see me now and then, that horrible feeling of being alone crept up on me again. Going to the health centre with Mitchell became the highlight of my week because it was the only time I'd see people. The nurse was as good as a stranger but she had become my only friend.

The loneliness became paralysing and I stopped wanting to get out of bed. The memories of Dave raping me returned and some mornings I wished I was dead. Mitchell was five months old when John said enough was enough.

'You need help, Tina,' he said, and cradled me like a baby. John had a temper but I had no doubt that he loved me.

'I think you should see a doctor,' he insisted.

'I thought everything would get better,' I sobbed.

'What are ya talking about?' John stroked the hair out of my eyes.

'I thought having a baby would help me forget about my old life.' I was crying so hard I couldn't breathe. 'I wanted to be the best mum.' I buried my head in John's chest. 'I wanted to give him what I never had.'

I'd been so hard on myself that I'd snapped. John was right, I needed help. I saw my doctor the next day and she diagnosed me with postnatal depression. I was given a course of antidepressants to help pull me through. Taking Prozac went against everything I had taught myself since I was six years old – to block off the pain, the fear and the loneliness. But I was scared that if I didn't, Mitchell could end up without a mother.

The drugs took a while to kick in but things were looking up within weeks. The thick fog that I woke up to every morning cleared and I saw sunshine again. Finding out I was pregnant again couldn't have come at a worse time.

'What d'ya mean, you're pregnant?' John gawped.

I'd had the coil fitted. It was the second time a contraceptive had let me down.

'I don't know what happened,' I said.

'Well, ya know I'll support ya, I always support ya,' he promised.

I was happy to give Mitchell a brother or sister but, to do so, I had to come off the antidepressants. I'd be opening Pandora's box again.

You can do it, Tina, you're a fighter.

17

Running Scared

'**M**um, I need your help,' I whispered down the phone. It was 2.30 a.m. I was hiding from John. I didn't have anyone else to call.

'Mum, John's headbutted me in the face.' I tried to stifle my tears.

'What?' she said. That woke her up.

'Where are ya?'

'I'm at home.'

'You've got to leave, now,' she insisted.

'I don't know if I can. I don't know if I'm strong enough.' I shook my head. I was the helpless child all over again, too scared to face my abuser.

Ten hours earlier.

'Leave it, John.' I guarded our front door with my new-born, Daniel, in my arms.

'Forget Steve, he's not worth it,' I said, trying to calm John down.

John had got into a row with his mate and he wanted to go back outside and give him a piece of his mind. They had both been drinking all day and I was acting as peace-keeper.

'Move out the way,' he slurred.

'No,' I snapped, clutching Daniel into my chest.

'Fucking, move, NOW!' he spat.

'NO.' I put my free hand on my hip, stubbornly. 'What's the point in having it out? You'll be friends again tomorrow. You're both just drunk,' I tried to reason.

'Fucking move!' His veins were popping in his fore-head.

I shook my head and he lurched forward.

SMACK. He headbutted me and my nose exploded. Blood splattered across the wall and poured over Daniel.

'Don't touch me!' I screamed at John.

I stumbled to the bathroom, leaving a trail of blood along the wall while still clutching Dan, protecting my baby. I laid him down on the sofa and cupped my nose as I crawled up the stairs. My face was burning with pain. I leant over the bath to contain the river of blood and caught a glimpse of my battered face in the mirror.

John had headbutted me so hard he had split the bridge of my nose open. My eyes were swollen and already turning black. I howled in agony, willing the bleeding to stop. John appeared at the bathroom door.

'I need to go to hospital!' I cried.

John looked at me blankly. There was no love left between us.

'OK,' he shrugged.

I had to drive myself to A&E, where I sat, alone, for

hours. I eventually got home at 1 a.m., with three stitches and a broken heart. I walked in to find John snoring on the sofa without a care in the world and I crept to the bedroom and cried silent tears.

God, please help me. Please take pity on me. I prayed for help just like when I was a girl.

I had no real friends, no family, I had no one to turn to. So I picked up the phone and called the woman who should have helped me all those years ago.

'That fucking monster!' Mum shouted, as I told her the story of what had happened.

'He didn't even care enough to stay awake for when I got back from the hospital,' I sobbed.

'Never mind that, it's the fact he's hit ya in the face. How could he do that to my daughter?' she raged.

It was ironic hearing her speak so passionately about someone hurting her daughter when the man sleeping next to her in bed had done far worse.

'Pack your bags and leave,' Mum insisted.

'Where am I going to go?' I whimpered.

'You can stay with me until you get yourself sorted.'

Bring my kids under the same roof as my stepdad. She must be joking.

'I'll work something out,' I tailed off.

'All right, love,' she said, and hung up.

I held the phone receiver into my chest for a moment. I wasn't ready to let go of my mum. Finally she was there for me, noticing me. Protecting me. If going through this pain with John meant I could have a mum, then maybe it was worth it.

I rang Romford Police Station the next day and asked to speak to the domestic violence unit. I'd had to report the assault at the hospital but I wasn't going to press charges – I was too scared to go through with a court case. I would accept their protection though, and the police arranged for me and my boys to be hidden in a refuge.

I spent the next few days carefully packing my and the kids' things into three large bags. I hid my secret under the stairs so John wouldn't cotton on but he was never one to miss a trick.

'What are ya doing?' he surprised me as I was scooping the photos off the mantelpiece.

'You made me jump,' I stammered, holding my chest like I was holding my heart from jumping out.

'I'm having a spring clean,' I lied.

'It's November.' He looked quizzical.

It was November 1997, Daniel was sixteen months old and Mitchell was nearly three. I remember it being very cold for the time of year and packing lots of winter woollies for the kids. I had no idea how long I was going to be in a safe house for. All I knew was that I had two black eyes and a swollen face whenever I looked in the mirror and I'd had enough. John had never lashed out at the boys but I'd made a promise to protect them from all harm, and seeing their mum get beaten up was harmful to their wellbeing. I'd grown up in a house where I watched Dave beat the crap out of Blake. Mum beat the crap out of me. I'd seen enough violence to last a lifetime.

I was whisked off to a refuge in Basildon while John was out at work. As I crossed town in the police car I imagined what his face would look like when he realised we'd gone. I'd been allocated Basildon because that's where Mum now lived with Dave and Jonathan. She'd promised me she'd be there to help me and the kids get through it, and I believed her.

Luckily we had a room to ourselves. I shared a bunk bed with Mitchell and Daniel had a cot. The walls were covered in scuff marks and the air was damp from the tears of all the women who had cried their eyes out in the room before me. I unzipped the bags and tried to make the kids feel at home. I didn't know where home was any more.

'I don't think I've ever had a place I could call home,' I whispered, tears welling in my eyes as I remembered the prison I grew up in.

The communal areas were clean, and I had my own cupboard in the kitchen to store food, but the whole set-up was grim. It reeked of pain and misery and I absorbed the other women's sadness as I sat watching TV with them until the early hours of the morning.

My mum became my saviour, visiting me every day. She smiled as she told me she was proud of me for leaving John. I fixated on the little things she did for me like they were grand gestures of love.

After ten days in the refuge I finally snapped. The kids were in bed and I was watching TV in the communal room. I had one eye on the screen and one ear listening into a conversation. A woman with mousey-coloured hair, wearing jogging bottoms and a jumper that drowned her fragile body, was crying as she told the story of why she was in hiding. Her face was puffy like a pillow from all the tears and I could feel her pain. She told how she'd moved halfway across the world to escape her husband, who had tried to kill her. I couldn't begin to imagine what she had been through. I decided I didn't belong there and called John the next day.

He met me in the Powerhouse pub in Basildon, with a hug and an armful of apologies.

'I'm sorry, babe.' He clutched my hands like I might vanish at any moment. 'I promise I'll never lay a finger on you again.' Tears trickled down his cheeks.

I wanted to believe him so much. I was scared to be alone. I wanted a family more than anything.

'I've missed you and the boys so much,' he said, his lip quivering.

I pressed my lips together as I thought it over.

'OK,' I whispered.

Life was good for the next two weeks as we prepared for Christmas together, and then John gave me a black eye as a present on Christmas Day. I found the courage in the New Year to leave him, and the magistrates' court served John with an injunction on 10 March 1998, to stop him coming anywhere near me or the boys.

We had twenty-four hours to pack our things and move to our temporary accommodation in Basildon. It was a beautiful house, with a huge front room, a fitted kitchen, a tiled bathroom and a master bedroom. Normal things to most people but it was the first time I had lived in a place I could call a 'home'.

Tears prickled my eyes but this time out of joy. I had my boys, I had my mum back, and I had a home. I was finally safe.

After we'd settled in I decided to call John to give him peace of mind. I didn't want to stop my children seeing their dad – he'd never laid a finger on them. He could have the boys twice a week, just as long as we met him in the town centre so our home was kept a secret, our sanctuary.

'Where the fuck are you?' He shouted so loudly I had to hold the receiver from my ear. I expected him to be angry but he was furious.

'Tell me where ya are, now,' he demanded.

'No, I will not tell you.' I trembled with fear. My body froze like when Dave used to touch me.

'You can see your boys but you are not welcome in our house any more,' I said, shaking.

'If you don't tell me where you are living . . .' He paused as he toyed with his threat. '. . . then I'm gonna tell your brothers what Dave did to ya,' he blackmailed.

It was like he'd stuck a knife into my stomach. I buckled forward with the thought of my brothers finding out about my dirty secret. I'd protected them from the truth for all these years. I'd sacrificed myself to protect them.

'Go on then, do it,' I hissed, and hung up.

Finally I'd stood up to him. I'd stood up to everyone who had pushed me into a silent corner. But within seconds the dread kicked in.

Oh, God, Mum is going to be so angry with me. She'll never forgive me.

I picked up the phone and dialled Mum, scared at the thought of losing her from my life again.

'Yeah, what's up?' she barked. I could hear the TV blaring in the background and I imagined her sprawled across the sofa.

'I just had a conversation with John,' I stuttered.

'Why did you ring him?' she shouted at me. 'You can start your life all over again, you don't need him,' she scolded.

'I . . .' but the words caught in my throat, I was the scared fourteen-year-old girl again, about to break the terrible news to my mum.

'John says he is going to tell Blake and Jonathan about what Dave did to me unless I tell him where we are living,' I blurted out.

There was a long icy silence.

'Well, you're going to have to tell him where you live then,' she said coldly.

What? She was willing to jeopardise my safety to protect my stepdad. Again. My heart sank like a stone to the ocean bed.

'I will not,' I said. 'This is about my boys. I don't want to tell him where I am.'

There was another long icy pause. I imagined her eyes narrowing.

'Well in that case I'll warn Blake and Jonathan that John is spreading vicious lies about their dad.'

She had it all worked out. She said it calmly like a killer plotting a murder. I wanted to shout, 'So that's it, you're sweeping it under the carpet again?' However, I couldn't get the words out. *She wasn't sorry at all. That apology letter had been a lie. It had all been a lie.*

I hung up and burst into tears.

I ended up telling John where we lived. Even though I hated Mum for betraying me again, the urge to win her approval came before any instinct to protect myself. She wasn't grateful for the sacrifice I made though, and we barely spoke for the next few months.

I was all alone, again.

I battered away my sad thoughts by trying to give my kids everything I never had. I became obsessively protective of them, watching their every move like a hawk. I couldn't erase my past but I could stop it happening again.

I was cleaning the house one evening when I got an electric shock from switching on the washing machine. The voltage sent me flying across the kitchen and I smacked my hand on the corner of the tiled wall as I crashed to the floor.

'What the . . .?' I said, shaking my head with confusion. I staggered to my feet and the pain shot up my arm like a bullet.

'Owww,' I screamed, clutching my hand in agony.

Everything around me turned into a messy blur and all I could hear was my heartbeat.

Ba-boom ba-boom.

In those few moments of shock, I thought about my mum. *I can use this to get her attention. I can call on her for help.*

SMACK. I whacked my hand on the corner of the wall.

If I make it worse, she'll have to help me.

SMACK SMACK.

She'll have to love me and protect me.

SMACK SMACK.

My hand was turning blue. I didn't feel the pain I was so angry.

SMACK SMACK.

That's for not protecting me, Mum.

CRACK. I broke my wrist.

I fell to the cold kitchen floor and sobbed uncontrollably. I curled my knees into my chest and rocked from side to side like a distressed animal. Luckily the boys were with their dad as it would have been like a horror film for them to see me like that.

I don't know how long I rocked and cried on that cold kitchen floor for, but eventually I managed to pull myself up and into my bedroom. I hid under my quilt like a child hiding from the world, clutching my throbbing arm. I could feel it swelling by the second but I was paralysed by sadness. I lay there all night in feverish sweats from the pain.

As day broke I picked up the phone by my bed. I should have called the doctor but then it would have all been for nothing.

'Mum, I need your help,' I said.

'Watcha done now?' She coughed on her morning cigarette.

'I've hurt my hand,' I started. 'I got an electric shock, which sent me flying against the wall.'

'You'll be all right.' Mum didn't do sympathy.

'I think it might be broken.' I pushed for a reaction.

'Whad'ya want me to do about it?'

'I'm going to need help driving to the hospital,' I pleaded.

There was a long, irritated pause.

'OK, I'll be over in a minute,' she sighed.

We barely spoke a word for those three hours she sat next to me in A&E, but just having her by my side was a great feeling. For those three hours it wasn't about Dave, or Blake, or Jonathan, it was about me. She was paying attention to me.

I had blood tests because the electric shock was so severe and I left hospital with my arm in a cast. Mum dropped me home and said she would do what she could to help me and the boys while I was out of action.

I smiled. Breaking my wrist had been worth it.

18

Risking It All

I dreaded Christmas. The thought of spending it on my own was paralysing. Loneliness scared me more than death and I would lie awake at night with butterflies in my stomach, imagining having no presents to open, no one to wish me 'Merry Christmas'. I hadn't made any friends in Basildon and Mum was the only person I spoke to apart from my neighbours, and John, when he collected the kids on Sundays.

'Why don't you bring the kids round here for Christmas,' Mum asked. It had been six months since I'd broken my wrist and we were speaking again.

'You can stay over Christmas Eve,' she said, filling my gobsmacked silence.

I hadn't spent the night in my family home since I was fifteen. I hadn't spoken to Dave since he tried to rape me again five years ago.

'No way,' I spluttered. 'Dave will be there, it's not a part of my life I want to revisit,' I said defiantly.

'Come on, he won't touch the children,' Mum said, like I was making a mountain out of a molehill.

I was speechless.

'They'll be in a room with you,' she went on, irritated by my concerns.

'No way,' I repeated.

'It just means you won't be on your own for Christmas,' she said, like she knew my greatest fear.

That horrible feeling of being alone sank in my stomach like a lead weight.

'You'll be lonely,' she continued, pressing my buttons.

'Where would we sleep?' I asked.

'In the spare room.'

Looking back now, it was one of the most stupid decisions I'd ever made, but at the time all I wanted was a family for Christmas. I wanted my mum.

'OK,' I said. She'd sold it to me.

I knew my boys would be safe because I'd protect them, but I was putting myself at risk because I felt that desperate.

As soon as we turned up at their house in Basildon it felt wrong. Mum opened the door and Dave was looming in the background. He looked even fatter and balder and stockier. He glanced at me and then dropped his eyes without as much as a hello.

You pathetic little man. I pity you.

Jonathan was watching Christmas TV and guzzling Cadbury's Roses chocolates, and Mum was getting irritated over holding the door open. The familiar smell of chip fat wafted into the street

'You coming in or what?' Mum barked.

This doesn't feel right; I don't want to be here.

'Yeah,' I mumbled. It was too late to change my mind. I was a fighter, I could get through the next twenty-four hours.

We spent Christmas Eve watching television and eating mince pies and chocolates. I didn't speak to Dave; we were like ships passing. There was an elephant in the room, which we pretended not to see for the sake of my kids and Jonathan. I dreaded bedtime but I had a plan worked out.

'Night,' I said to Mum as I lifted Daniel into my arms. Mitchell was nearly four now and toddled along beside me. I didn't even look at Dave as I headed to the spare room. There was no lock on the door but that was OK, I was going to use the weight of my body as a doorstop.

The mattress made a scratching noise like nails on a black-board as I pulled it across the floor and pushed it up against the door. The boys were both still in nappies so I didn't have to worry about letting them out to use the loo. I wrapped them snugly in quilts and then lay across the doorway like a dog guarding its master.

I never properly let my body sleep, as my ears pricked at the slightest sound: the TV blare being silenced; the final clink of the whisky glass on the coffee table. The familiar noises that meant Dave was getting ready for bed. I held my breath as I listened to his footsteps along the hallway. He ran the tap and brushed his teeth and I imagined his lecherous eyes checking himself out in the mirror. My body was rigid as I braced myself for the push on the door handle.

Boom boom, my heart was hammering.

The house turned ghostly silent and I panicked. *Where is he? Can I hear him breathing outside my door?*

CLICK, went the door on Mum's bedroom. He had gone to bed. I was safe, for now. I dozed in and out of a light sleep, jolting awake at every creak. I should have guessed I would have been hit with a tornado of memories. I remembered the sound of Dave closing my bedroom door after he had visited me in the night. I remembered the noise of the lid being twisted off the pot full of creamy liquid. I could smell Old Spice in my room. I could smell him.

I could hear 'Merry Christmas Everyone' blaring on the radio from Mum's bedroom.

'Merry Christmas,' I whispered to my boys and kissed them both on their sleepy heads. I'd gone to town with presents this year – I wanted to give them what I never had. I'd spent days wrapping them and I couldn't wait to see their little faces light up under the tree.

I could smell Brussels sprouts and lard wafting into the living room. Mum was doing her usual half-hearted cooking, with one eye on the pots and another on the TV, still wrapped in her dressing gown.

'Merry Christmas,' I said, giving her a kiss on the cheek.

'Merry Christmas, Jonathan,' I shouted over to my brother on the sofa. Blake was with his new wife, Sue, for the day.

I ignored Dave. It was like he didn't exist. He didn't try to talk to me either, probably out of fear of what I might say. He was a coward.

'Do you want a hand, Mum?' I asked, feeling the tension.

You could have cut the air in that living room with a knife.

'Yeah,' she grunted, and then handed the bulk of the cooking over to me.

I kept my boys by my side the whole time, so Dave couldn't touch them. If Dave was on one side of the room, I'd be on the other. I kept them constantly amused so they wouldn't crawl to Dave for attention. By the time I drove home I felt like I'd been battered in a storm – exhausted from keeping my guard up for twenty-four hours. I tucked my boys into bed and then flopped down on the sofa, my belly full of turkey and roast potatoes and stuffing.

Although every tired bone in my body was screaming *sleep*, my head was telling me to get up and get showered. Being back in their house, with *him*, had made me feel dirty. I needed to scrub away the horrific memories.

Up Tina. Move. I scrubbed my skin until it was pink and sore.

I had a quiet New Year, and then the letter arrived. My name wasn't written in swirly handwriting this time, but in neat printed typeface with an ominous Basildon County Council stamp.

Social services requests Miss Tina Renton to attend a meeting on 21 January 1999 regarding the welfare of your sons Mitchell and Daniel.

My eyes nearly popped out of my head.

John must have found out I'd taken the boys to my mum's for Christmas and reported me to Social Services. He must have told them I'd been abused as a child and I'd compromised our children's safety by taking them into the perpetrator's house. I shook my head with disbelief. I couldn't believe he'd grassed on me.

But I was angrier at myself. The letter had brought me back into the real world. *Why the hell did I do that? It was just a day. I should never have taken my kids around there. Stupid, Tina, stupid.* I smacked my legs with my fists.

My boys meant everything to me; they were all I had in the world. I picked up the phone and called Mum.

'They're going to take my kids away,' I cried as soon as she answered.

'What? Who?'

'Social Services. John told them about Dave.' I was trembling with fear.

'Oh, for fuck's sake,' she spat.

'What am I going to do?' I begged for her help.

'You're going to keep calm. He's not going to take your kids,' she promised.

Her words fell on deaf ears and all I wanted to do was punish myself for being so stupid. I had terrible nightmares as I counted down the days until the hearing.

I dreamt I had to choose between my boys. Dirty water splattered up my shins as I ran through a dark tunnel. I was holding Daniel and Mitchell, and my arms felt like they were going to tear out of their sockets.

Splash. I could hear him getting closer.

Splash. It was too dark to see his face but I could see the edge of his knife, glinting.

The trickle of water down the slimy walls was as loud as my heartbeat.

'Help!' I screamed. But no one could hear me. I was so far underground.

'Somebody help me!' My voice felt like splinters in my throat.

I couldn't carry both the boys, they were too heavy. I turned around and his knife was at my throat.

'Choose which one lives and which one dies,' he laughed.

'No!' I screamed, clutching my boys into my chest.

I woke up hugging my pillow, dripping in sweat. I threw my quilt to the ground and darted into my boys' bedroom. They were OK, they were sleeping like babies.

'Oh, thank God,' I whispered, holding my heart with my hands. I could feel it galloping under my shaking fingers. I'd suffered from the worst nightmares since Dave started touching me but I had never dreamt about my kids. *Thank God my mum will be at the meeting to protect me.*

Mum was wearing her usual T-shirt, calf-length skirt and black handbag slung over her shoulder when I picked her up the next morning. She never wore anything else, come rain or shine. I'd done my best to look smart, pinning my long hair back into a ponytail and squeezing into a fitted pair of trousers. Usually I never wore tight clothes as I'd never stopped hating my body.

We were led through the bland corridors of Ely House, the Social Services offices, to our meeting. John was already sat at the large oval table, which was too big for the room. I glared at him and he eyeballed me back. There were half-a-dozen official-looking people there watching me, as I squeezed myself around the table to my allocated seat. The central heating was turned up so high I couldn't breathe.

'Can we open a window in here, please,' I asked aggressively. I didn't want them to see my fear.

'Miss Renton, we've brought you here today because a complaint has been made against you,' said a woman wearing a badly fitting grey trouser suit. I shot John a look of disgust. I took a gulp of water as I waited for them to drop the bombshell.

'We understand you have a history of abuse,' the lady said matter-of-factly. 'That you were abused by your stepfather.'

I squirmed in my chair. I'd never heard those words spoken out loud before, let alone by a stranger. I felt sick. I turned to Mum for support but she was too busy snarling at John. *Look at me. Goddammit, look at ME*.

'And we understand you took your children ...' The woman paused to consult her notes. '... your children Mitchell and Daniel for Christmas at your stepfather's house.'

I stared at her like a rabbit caught in headlights.

'Miss Renton, is it true that you have been abused?' she asked.

Oh, God, I wanted to be sick.

'Who were you abused by, Miss Renton?' she pushed.

'By her stepfather, David Moore,' John shouted.

I burst into tears.

'How could you let that sicko anywhere near our kids?' He lifted out of his chair.

'Please stop,' I sobbed.

'He's a paedophile,' John shouted.

'Please,' I wailed. I could have been sitting there naked, I felt so exposed.

'Let's take a five-minute break,' the woman interrupted, pushing John back into his chair.

I ran out of the room and Mum came after me. I turned to her like a little girl wanting a hug of reassurance. *Hug me please hug me*. But Mum didn't do sympathy. She stood there studying me with her glacial eyes.

'I can't do this,' I blubbered, drying my tears with my sleeve.

'Just deny it,' Mum spat.

'What?' I looked at her with disbelief.

'Deny it.' She looked at me like I was thick.

I couldn't believe she was brushing it under the carpet, again. After all these years she still didn't understand how she had betrayed me. She didn't see how Dave had destroyed my life.

'No, I won't deny it,' I said, and slung my hands on my hips, pretending to be brave.

'For God's sake, tell them you made it up,' she shouted down the corridor. 'That way there will never be an issue.'

Tears streamed down my face. I didn't care who saw me, I was so distressed.

'I'm not going to deny it, because it's *true*,' I whimpered.

Mum threw up her arms in frustration.

'But you're going to open a big can of worms. Even if you

don't want to bring the boys over any more, deny it, because it's going to cause so much trouble.'

'You mean it's going to cause *you* so much trouble,' I said, and pointed my finger angrily at her. 'This isn't about you. This isn't even about me. This is about my children and they will always come first.' I broke down sobbing. I turned my back on her. I couldn't bear to look at her face. I took three deep breaths and stormed back into the meeting room, leaving her standing in the corridor.

'Are you OK, Miss Renton,' the lady asked, as I dabbed my puffy eyes.

'Yes,' I said, pulling out a chair. I heard the door click behind me as Mum followed me in.

'John is correct about what he has said. I was a victim of child abuse by my stepfather,' I announced.

I heard my mum gasp next to me.

'I'm happy to sign this agreement to say I'll never let my children come into contact with David Moore again,' I said, and picked up the pen next to my hand.

I could feel Mum's eyes boring into me but I didn't care, she'd only let me down again. She'd proven to me, yet again, she would rather protect Dave, and herself, than me.

What more could I do to make her love me?

The meeting was closed and I sprinted for the door to avoid a confrontation with John. Mum trailed behind like a sulky kid as we headed to the car, muttering under her breath. I kept my armour on but it was getting painfully heavy.

There was only a gearstick between us in the car but there

may as well have been a continent because she was so distant. How could she be angry at me? Did she really expect me to say sorry? I dropped her off without a word and then my dam of strength broke. I could barely see the road home through my blur of tears.

'Damn you, Mum!' I shouted. She'd done it again. By ignoring me, by being horrible to me, Mum had made me feel like I was in the wrong. The more she ignored me the more I craved her love.

I'll call her tomorrow and tell her how sorry I am.

19

Finding My Voice

'Mummy, I'm sorry,' Mitchell whimpered.

'It's too late for that. You can never go back. Now get out of my sight before I kill ya!' I shouted.

I was furious. After all the hard work I'd put into fighting for my kids, Mitchell had got expelled from school. I'd been called into the headmistress's office that morning to hear how my ten-year-old son had been in a scuffle with the deputy head.

'He had been asked to work through his lunch hour because he'd misbehaved in class, again,' Mrs McCutcheon explained as she pressed her hands together.

She described how Mitchell had made a run for the class-room door. The deputy head grabbed him and they both fell backwards onto the floor, and she had hit her head in the scuffle.

I sunk my head into my hands as I'd lost count of how many times I'd been called into the headmistress's office over the past year. Bunking off class, refusing to take part in class, climbing a tree on the school field and refusing to come down – Mitchell had been a terror. Where had I failed him?

The past few years had been much calmer now John was out of my life. I'd screwed up my education because of Dave, so I wanted my boys to go to university and make something of themselves.

I picked up the phone in anger and dialled the school.

'I'd like to appeal against the decision to exclude my son Mitchell,' I announced. 'And can I have all of Mitchell's school records please?'

'You'll have to pay for those, Miss Renton,' the school secretary replied.

'Fine,' I said. Mitchell was no angel but I'd made a promise to protect my boys and I wasn't going to let this go without a fight.

I'd grown a little in confidence over the past few years, as I'd studied to become a mental-health counsellor in my spare time. The diploma had taught me to stand up for what I believed in. To help people who didn't have a voice. I needed to stand up for Mitchell now.

The photocopied notes arrived in the post a couple of days later in a sun-bleached sleeve, held together by an elastic band. I sighed deeply as I looked at the mountain of pages. I didn't even know what I was looking for. *What was I doing?*

I waited for the kids to go to bed and then I poured myself a strong cup of coffee before pulling up a chair at the kitchen table. I opened the file and started wading through the paperwork. 'Disruptive behaviour', 'difficulty in concentrating', my eyes grew heavy as I ploughed on.

I rested my head into my hand and turned the page. More

'difficulty concentrating in class'. *Why is my boy struggling to concentrate?* My eyelids felt like lead. They rolled down like shutters and the words on the page were now floating letters in darkness.

'Mummy, wake up.' I was jolted from my dream by Mitchell.

My neck was killing me – I'd fallen asleep at the table with my arm for a pillow.

'What are you doing up, love?' I asked, massaging my neck. I checked the clock on the cooker, it was 1.32 a.m.

'I was worried because I didn't hear you go to bed,' he said, shivering in his pyjamas. It was January and freezing. I could tell he was worried I was still angry at him but I could never stay mad at my boys.

'Get to bed or you'll catch your death,' I said, patting him away. 'Mummy just needs to finish doing a bit more work.'

Mitchell gave me a kiss goodnight and then scuttled back into his bedroom. I wrapped a scarf around my neck and turned the page. I still had three years to cover. More notes, more bad handwriting that I could barely read. My eyelids started to roll down again.

'Hang on a minute, what's this?' I mumbled. It was a small note in the margin – blink and I would have missed it:

Bs and Ds back to front. Dyslexia?

The school had suspected Mitchell was dyslexic three years ago and had done nothing about it? Anger burnt in the pit of my stomach. I'd gone from three-quarters asleep to wide awake in a split second. I poured myself another cup of coffee and started on the remaining years – taking notes, circling, highlighting – I was the most determined I had ever been in my life.

I finally made it to bed when the birds were waking up. I caught a couple of hours sleep before I was up again getting Daniel ready for school. I was running on adrenalin and loving it.

'Mitchell, Mummy won't be angry, I just need you to tell me the truth,' I said, shaking cereal into Dan's bowl.

'Do you find it hard to read books?' I asked gently.

He looked at me blankly.

'Do you find it hard to spell words?'

Mitchell dropped his head like he was ashamed.

'I guess so,' he shrugged.

'Mummy, is Mitchell stupid?' Dan piped up with a mouth full of cornflakes and milk.

'No, Dan, don't call your brother stupid. And don't talk with your mouth full,' I scolded him.

'It's OK, Mitchell, it's not your fault.' I cuddled my eldest in my arms.

Out of the little money I had, I paid for Mitchell to have a dyslexia test. The result came back that he was severely dyslexic.

'I bloody knew it,' I said as I held the report in my hands. 'And that school knew it three years ago but didn't do anything about it.'

'They are going to wish they never expelled you,' I said, turning to Mitchell triumphantly. I'd found a confidence I never knew I had and I'd found a brain I'd never put to the test before.

I appealed before the school's board of governors in the second week of February 2005, a few weeks after Mitchell had been expelled. Under my arm I carried my weapon – a report I'd prepared from what I'd pulled from Mitchell's file. I wore a suit jacket to finish the look.

I'd asked Mum to come with me so she could take notes using her secretarial shorthand skills. I was too focused that day to take any notice of her mutterings and put-downs about it being a waste of time. My heart was galloping by the time we were called inside the meeting room.

I'd never stood up in front of a room full of people before. I'd spent my life hiding in the shadows, hating myself and what I looked like. I was at one end of the oval table with my mum, and at the other was the headmistress, three governors and a skinny-looking guy from the Local Education Authority. I looked across to my mum and she looked bored. Her blue eyes had frozen over.

One of the governors cleared her throat to commence the meeting.

'We are here today because Ms Renton is appealing against the school's decision to permanently exclude her son, Mitchell. Mrs McCutcheon, would you be so kind as to start us off by explaining your decision.' The governor smiled.

Mrs McCutcheon pressed her hands together and started to tell her side of the story. She had a sweet, soft voice, not the sort you'd expect to come out of a stern headmistress's mouth. Mum was scribbling notes; her shorthand of lines and dots looked like a foreign language.

'Are you ready, Ms Renton?' The governor signalled me to take the floor.

No, I'm petrified.

'Yes,' I lied. I could feel beads of sweat on the back of my neck. I thought about protecting my boy and a bullet of adrenalin shot through my veins.

'I feel that this school has failed my son,' I announced. 'I feel that the school failed him because you didn't pick up on the fact that my son has a learning disability,' I said, rising to my feet. Inside I was shaking.

'See for yourself. Here's his report.' I pushed it across the table.

'As you can see, his dyslexia was noticed years ago but the school did nothing about it,' I said, my hands on my hips.

'You weren't offering him any classroom support.' I went on to list a hundred and one things that the school could have done to help.

'If you had done this, if you had helped my son, then things would have been different. Mitchell behaved in the way he did because he wasn't getting the support he needed and I feel the school failed him.' I took a deep breath, I'd forgotten to breathe.

A stunned silence choked the room.

'OK, let's break for a moment,' the governor stepped in.

The sound of chairs scraping backwards was like nails on a board. We were led into a room while the governors made their decision over a cup of tea and bourbon biscuits. Mum quickly took a seat. She wasn't one to stand when she didn't have to. I heard a quiet knock and in walked the guy from the LEA. He had a grin across his face like something had amused him.

'That was the best parental representation I have ever seen,' he said. It felt like he wanted to clap.

'Thanks,' I muttered, embarrassed.

'Have you considered being a lawyer?' he said, narrowing his eyes with sincerity.

'Uh, no.' I laughed. I'd dreamt of being a lawyer when I was a kid but I didn't think I was clever enough.

But just a flippant comment like that can change your life.

I walked back into that meeting room with a skip in my step. The chairing governor cleared her throat again and announced that they had decided to back Mrs McCutcheon's decision to expel my son.

Damn it. I clenched my fists in anger under the table.

'Thank you,' I said, rising to my feet. 'I'll be taking this forward to the Statutory Board of Appeals.' I was like a dog with a bone. I shook hands and then left with Mum in tow.

'Well, I could have told ya that would be a waste of time,' Mum grumbled.

'No, it wasn't. I'm going to fight this all the way. I have a valid case,' I snapped.

Did you ever think about being a lawyer? The words circled in my head.

Nah, I could never be a lawyer. I shook the thought away and carried on walking to my car.

20

A Degree of Change

I plastered my hand over my mouth to hold in my giggles. Why is it that you always want to laugh at the most inappropriate moments? The lecture hall was as quiet as a library except for me, and my new friends, Amanda and Louise, who were trying to stifle their sniggers in the second row from the front.

Louise made the weirdest sound when she held in her laughter, like she was a pressure cooker about to blow. I looked at Amanda out of the corner of my eye and she was shaking behind her textbook. It was too much, I erupted like a volcano, giggle spit spraying from my mouth, snot running from my nose.

'Would you like to tell the class what is so funny?' the lecturer said, holding the microphone to my mouth.

'Nothing,' I mumbled, my cheeks turning crimson with embarrassment. I didn't know what we were laughing at, we'd just set each other off like dominoes.

The LEA guy's comment turned out to be less throwaway than I first thought. I couldn't shake his words out of my head and in October 2006 I started a law degree at Essex University. I fought my way there by completing an access course at the same time as winning my son's appeal at the council's Statutory Board. I'd found a brain that I never realised I had. I'd found my voice.

I'd also finally found some friends. Amanda had given up her high-flying job to study law. She was the same age as me, thirty-one , helping me feel a little less self-conscious about being one of the only mature students on the course. Louise was twenty-one, and a bundle of fun. She had dark-blonde hair with bright blonde highlights to mimic her colourful personality. We quickly formed a study group that would meet in the last booth of the Blues Café to dissect our lectures.

'I can't get my head around this flow chart,' I said, gritting my teeth. Like Mitchell, I'd been diagnosed with dyslexia while I was completing my access course. I found it hard to read and I would have to go over chapters several times before it stuck.

'Nothing another cup of coffee won't help.' Amanda grinned, pushing her glasses back up her nose. We must have spent half our student loans on coffee and cake in that first term.

'Go on then,' I nudged Louise. It was her turn to do the coffee run. I smiled to myself as I took it all in. Never in a million years would I have dreamt I'd make it to university when I sat on my mum's bed that night and told her about Dave. I'd been made to believe I was good for nothing except being my stepfather's plaything. *You're not clever enough to do that. Give up now.* I could hear my mum's words in my head, putting me down.

Well, look at me now, Mum.

'They were out of scones so I got you a cookie,' Louise said, coming back with a tray full of calories.

'You bad girl, you know I'm on a diet,' I teased her. I'd been watching my weight for the past year, dropping from eighteen stone to fourteen. I was looking so transformed even my mum noticed. I was feeling good about myself for the first time since I don't know when. The bad dreams had stopped. The sad feeling in my gut had lifted.

I'd get home in the evenings exhausted, but buzzing from all the information I'd learnt that day. We now lived in Colchester so my boys could go to a school that specialised in dyslexia. And I'd met someone. Someone who put *me* first.

It felt like I'd been single for an eternity when I met Gary Briggs on an Internet dating site. I was so protective of my boys I was reluctant to let anyone into my house, into my heart, but Gary was such a natural with my kids it was like he had always been part of our lives. He took them to the park rollerblading, he played computer games with them and they adored him.

Within four months Gary had moved in. Because he had just gone through a bitter divorce he'd cut ties with lots of his wife's friends and didn't know many people in Colchester. I became the centre of his life and I loved being put first. It felt like me and him versus the world the way we did everything together, just the two of us. I loved our Friday cinema nights and Sundays under the duvet watching DVDs.

Even though Gary was my age, and had a serious job, working in the control room of a security company, he acted like a kid.

I couldn't hear anything in the shower, when the water rained into my ears. I left the bathroom door open as usual – a hangover from hating the way my stepfather closed my bedroom door – and Gary used that as his cue.

'*Arrrgh!*' I screamed with fright as he pulled back the shower curtain.

Gary was holding a glass full of water and ice cubes and wearing a big grin on his face.

'Don't you bloody dare,' I squealed, hiding behind the curtain.

He roared with laughter and then tipped the freezing water over my cowering body.

'You're going to pay for that,' I yelled, bounding out of the shower like a tiger. I chased him around the living room, in just a towel.

'Too slow,' he taunted. I ran into the kitchen, dipped the end of a tea towel in water and then came back, armed with my whip.

CRACK! I sliced through the air with my tea towel.

'Missed,' he teased.

CRACK! right on the bum.

'*Owww,*' he yelped in pain.

'Gotcha,' I said, then leapt on him in a fit of giggles.

We were like two kids running around without a care in the world. I'd never had a childhood, but with Gary I could be a kid again. I can't remember ever play-fighting when I was growing up, I was too busy cooking and cleaning and having real fights with Blake and Mum.

Gary was a good-looking bloke. Tall, blond, blue eyes. He was very skinny though, and the first time I laid eyes on him I thought we could never have a sexual relationship because I'd snap him in two. The chemistry was there though, and I could relax in bed with him. There were some things I hated doing, like oral sex. It reminded me of my stepdad thrusting himself into my mouth, so deep I couldn't breathe. I hated him kissing me 'down there' because it reminded me of *his* slimy tongue. I couldn't tell Gary though. How could I tell him the truth? He would never look at me in the same way again. He'd probably dump me and then I'd lose the family I'd finally found.

I also hated my body. Play-fighting was a one-off – I'd usually wrap my arms over my breasts when I got out of bed.

'Don't cover yourself up,' Gary pleaded as I backed out of the bedroom door so he wouldn't see my bum.

'I'm shy,' I smiled coyly.

Your leering eyes make my skin crawl.

'You're gorgeous,' he said and beckoned me back to bed.

I'm hideous.

'I'll be back in a minute.' I scurried to the bathroom.

I tried so hard to keep a normal family life while studying for my degree. I'd come home, cook dinner, put the kids to bed, spend time with Gary and then study until 11 p.m. I'd get up at 6 a.m., prepare dinner for that evening, get the kids ready for school, and then head to campus.

But like everything good in my life – it turned to shit.

'What's up with you, babe?' Louise asked as she hugged her fourth cup of coffee in our favourite café.

'Ah nothing.' I shrugged. I was used to keeping my troubles to myself.

'That means everything,' Amanda said, and raised her eyebrows.

'It's Gary. He's become possessive, checking my phone, questioning me about every move I make. I think he's jealous about the amount of time I'm putting into my degree. It's like he's threatened by my success.'

'Men!' Amanda threw her arms in the air out of exasperation.

'He says he never gets to spend time with me,' I went on.

'You've fought so hard to get here, are you going to give that up for a guy?' Amanda said, leaning across the table.

'But I love him.' My lip trembled.

Amanda and Louise shook their heads in protest.

Having a family meant more to me than anything in the world, but as the fighting with Gary got worse, I did something I'd never done before. I put my career before a guy. A fire was burning inside me to make something of my life and I was determined to become a lawyer. I wanted to show my boys what to aim for. I wanted to make my mum proud and show my mum I was worthy of her love.

A month into my second year at uni, I found the courage to break it off with Gary. A few weeks later, as the dreaded

Christmas approached, I thought I'd cut my nose off to spite my face.

'Why don't you spend Christmas at ours?' Mum said, sprawled on a hospital bed. She was recovering from pneumonia and I was the only one in the family who could be bothered to look after her.

'The boys are with John this year, you'll be all on your own,' she coughed.

She still knew how to press my buttons even when she was at death's door.

'Blake is coming around with his wife Sue, Jonathan will be there, we'll be family.'

That word, *family*, was like a javelin through my heart. *How dare she throw it around like she knew what it meant?*

But we hadn't been a family since I left at fifteen. I conjured up this starry-eyed vision of us all sitting around the table with our cracker hats on, laughing at the bad jokes and having seconds of mushy sprouts and Yorkshire pudding. I also felt, despite all the times she had let me down, I must look after my mum because she was poorly. It was my time to shine, another chance to show her how good a daughter I could be.

'OK.' I nodded.

I arrived with a bagful of gifts and high hopes that this year would be different. Blake was now in his thirties, married, surely he was too old to start a fight with me? Jonathan was now twenty-one and I loved him for being the baby of the family, the little brother I took care of when he was tiny. I could put up with my stepdad for twelve hours, if it meant I had my mum and my brothers back.

'Hey, look, it's our adopted sister,' Blake joked as I turned up on the doorstep.

'Ha ha, very funny.' I pretended to take it on the chin. Inside, it hurt like hell. It had been my brother's running joke for years because they said I was nothing like the rest of the family.

'Merry Christmas.' I gave Blake and his wife Sue a kiss on the cheek.

'Merry Christmas, Jonathan.' Kiss.

Mum was in her dressing gown, her skin ashen and her eyes bloodshot.

'Merry Christmas, Mum.' I gave her a loving kiss.

I looked at Dave and he looked at me and then we looked away. *Did my brothers ever wonder why I barely spoke to Dave?* Sue handed me a glass of Baileys liqueur and I took a large glug to calm my nerves. It was going to be harder to pretend everything was normal than I had thought.

'Better get started on the dinner then?' I rolled my eyes to Sue.

'Another Baileys?' Sue asked.

'Girl after my own heart,' I laughed, holding out my glass.

I was half cut as I prepared the roast parsnips, potatoes and turkey. The boys and Mum watched TV. I couldn't bring myself to look at Dave. The drunker I got, the sadder I felt.

'Dinner's served.' I belched.

'About time,' Blake grumbled. He hadn't changed a bit, except he was tubbier. Sue seemed like a nice girl; I wanted to ask her what the hell she saw in my brother.

We popped crackers and passed the meat around the table. Blake, Mum and Jonathan filled up their plates to the brim, gravy spilling over onto their mats. Everyone took it in turns to read their jokes and even Mum cracked a smile.

I don't belong here.

The thought hit me like a bolt of lightning as I watched them all laughing and stuffing their faces. My brothers had no idea who the man they call their dad really was. They had no idea about the dirty secret that had been swept under the carpet for over twenty years.

You have no idea what I sacrificed to protect you and keep a roof over your heads.

I felt my eyes get full with tears. I looked away for a second to blink them away. I was relieved to clear the table for pudding and took another desperate swig of Baileys in the kitchen.

When dinner was over, the guys scampered off to the living room, leaving Sue and I to clear up. I drew on a smile and joined the rabble in the lounge. After all, it wasn't Blake and Jonathan's fault that I had to put on a charade. My eyes locked on Dave instantly, like a heat-seeking missile. He was slumped in the armchair by the tele, his full belly rolling over his cream chino trousers.

Sue went to sit next to Blake on the two-seater sofa. He casually threw his arm around her and she cuddled into him. There was a space for me next to Mum, between her and Jonathan on the three-seater.

'Can you move your feet,' I asked Jonathan, who had his feet across my place.

'Piss off,' he snarled. 'Sit on the floor.'

He may as well have punched me in the stomach. My little brother, who I'd raised like my own, was telling me to take a seat on the floor because he wanted his feet up. I looked around the room but everyone had pretended not to hear.

Or they just didn't care what happened to me.

I bit my lip to stop the tears. I dropped my head like a beaten dog and found my basket on the floor by the fireplace. I pulled my knees into my chest like I used to do when I was a child. God it was uncomfortable.

I felt like a ghost because everyone looked through me like I wasn't there. I could see them though – four beached whales sprawled across the lounge. Poor Sue, if only she had known what she was marrying into. I wished I had never gone round there.

Mum's phone ringing broke into my bitter thoughts.

'Hello?' she grunted. 'Oh, hiya, Simon.'

It was her boss.

Blake and Jonathan carried on their conversation over her.

'You're fucking joking, no fucking way,' Jonathan laughed loudly. 'That's fucking funny.' Every other word was a swearword.

'Oi – shhhh,' me and Sue said simultaneously, pointing to Mum on the phone.

Jonathan's head shot around to glare at me. His eyes were cold and mean.

'Who the fuck do you think you are?' he sneered.

What? I was stunned.

'No one wants you here anyway. Why don't you just fuck off,' he said, dismissing me with his hand.

My jaw dropped to the ground. I felt like a piece of shit. I grabbed my keys and ran out the front door to my car. I'd drunk too much Baileys to drive – goddammit. I bashed my hands on the steering wheel in anger and then the dam of tears I'd been holding in all day broke. I buried my head into my arms and sobbed.

I was the one who got raped, so why am I the one being punished for it?

'I just want a family, I just want a family,' I whispered through my tears.

I jumped as the side door was flung open, letting in an Arctic breeze.

'Are you all right?' Sue asked, tentatively putting her hand on my back.

'No, I'm not,' I said, scratching the tears away with my sleeve. 'I didn't deserve that. You said exactly the same thing to Jonathan but he attacked me.'

Sue nodded. I could tell she wasn't the confrontational type; you couldn't be to marry my brother, I thought.

'What are you going to do?' she asked limply.

'I dunno,' I said, resting my head on the steering wheel. 'I can't go anywhere. Guess I'm going to have to sit it out.'

Sue shivered and then left me in the car with my thoughts. I sat there for half an hour, ploughing through my feelings of rejection. *I've had it with my brothers. As far as I'm concerned I am adopted. They can go screw themselves. Now buck up, Tina, and show them that they can't get the better of you.*

I slammed the car door and marched back into the house. Mum's face was braced for an argument. Jonathan had scurried upstairs to avoid me.

'Go easy on him, love. He's had a really bad time with work.' Mum smiled but her eyes were as cold as ice.

'All both of you do is protect him,' I blasted. It was the truth on so many levels. Dave was in the kitchen so he would have heard me. I wanted him to hear.

You could have cut the air with a knife from the tension. I backed off and grabbed my laptop – it was Christmas after all, I didn't want to be blamed for ruining that too. I found a spot on the sofa and booted up my computer, the familiar 'Welcome' noise was my only comfort. The argument was brushed under the carpet and everyone watched TV and ate chocolates, while I messaged strangers on an Internet chatroom.

Here I am, sitting in a room with my family, talking to strangers on the Internet. That's how alienated I feel.

I kept my steel armour on until bedtime, when it came crashing to the floor in a river of tears. Loneliness is like depression: until you suffer from it, you don't know how hard it is to pull yourself out of it. It's a paralysing feeling that gnaws at your heart.

I pulled at the mattress and pushed it in front of the door like a barricade. *He* wasn't going to touch me tonight. I pulled the duvet up to my chin and thought about my kids, if they were OK without me. I missed them so much. This will be the last Christmas I spend without them, I swore.

I was out of bed before the birds could wish me 'good morning'.

'Don't go,' Mum whined as I opened the front door.

'I don't want to be where I'm not wanted,' I replied, walking to my car.

How many times can you get kicked in the teeth before you cry enough is enough? I was about to find out.

21

Shock to the System

'Is that Tina?' said a man's voice I didn't recognise.

I was holding my mobile phone to my ear with my shoulder while I packed my shopping at the supermarket checkout. I hadn't recognised the number that flashed up on my screen.

'Yeah.' I furrowed my brow.

'My name is Stuart . . .' He spoke slowly, like he was talking to a child. 'I don't want you to panic, but I'm with your son, Daniel, at the moment, and there has been a bit of an accident . . .'

There was a dramatic pause, like they do on game shows before they tell the contestants they've got through to the next round.

'He's been run over.'

I dropped my four shopping bags.

I was two weeks away from my second-year exams when I got the phone call on 14 April 2008. Suddenly, all the things I'd been struggling with – the terrible Christmas I'd had with my family, the hours I'd spent studying and writing essays – became insignificant. All I could imagine was my son lying dead across a road.

'Is this a joke?' I stuttered. I wanted him to tell me it was a wind-up.

'No, I'm serious,' Stuart carried on in his calm voice. 'He's been hit by a car. I'm a first-aider. I was walking past when it happened.'

'Is he OK? Can I speak to him!' I shrieked.

'He's unconscious,' Stuart explained.

I was going to be sick. The noise of the checkout bleep was now like a drill into my brain.

Shut up, shut up.

'I've got your other son with me. An ambulance has been called.'

'Can I speak to my other son?' I asked calmly.

It was like we were having a conversation on a slow-motion setting. My mouth felt heavy as I held on to the words. The trolleys and shopping bags and special-offer signs smudged into a blur. I dropped what I was doing and walked away from the till.

'Hello? Excuse me?' shouted the confused checkout lady. Her voice faded into an echo.

I clutched the phone as I waited for Mitchell to be put on the line. He was sobbing. I could feel his distress through the receiver.

'Are you all right?'

I couldn't hear his reply through his howling.

'Listen, boy, where are you?' I pressed him for answers.

'By the ...' He tried to speak. 'By the water tower in Brightlingsea ...' he heaved '... by our school.'

'OK, babe, I'm on my way. I'm in Colchester but I'll be

there in a minute.' I hung up, my hands shaking. I couldn't bear to hear my baby cry and not be there to help him. *How could this happen?* I hated myself for not being able to protect them.

I drove off but then the shock hit me like a train. I pulled over into a lay-by, my whole body shaking. *What do I do now? Drive to Colchester General Hospital? Or to Brightlingsea and beat the ambulance?* I shook my head in turmoil, unable to make a decision, to make sense of what had happened. I must have looked like a zombie to anyone passing by.

I started up the ignition; I was going to beat the ambulance. I cried the whole way as I sped along the narrow country roads to the seaside town.

Neee Naaaw Neee Naaaw.

The ambulance came flying up behind me with its blues and twos on just as I reached the brow of the hill. I pulled over and let it pass and then followed its dust trail. I was speeding, I couldn't see the road for my tears, but I would do whatever it took to get to my boys.

I parked behind the ambulance. School kids were running around everywhere like ants and I couldn't see Dan. I took a deep breath and prepared myself for the worst.

Pull yourself together, Tina, you can't let your kids see you like this.

I dried my tears and charged forward. A policeman darted in front of me, barricading my way with his body.

'That's my son!' I screamed, breaking through his arms.

'Stop!' he shouted behind me but it was too late. It looked like a scene out of the TV show *Casualty*. Daniel was slumped with his back against the wall, blood pouring down his face, out of his nose, out of his ear. He looked so fragile, like a broken doll. Mitchell ran out in front of me, crying. I grabbed his shoulders and shook him gently.

'Look, son, I know you need me, but your brother needs me more right now. Just give me a minute and I'll be right back with you.' I looked him in the eye. He nodded, his bottom lip quivering.

I crouched down beside Dan, who was now conscious. His elbows were swollen to the size of tennis balls, he had a gash above his eyes and he was caked in mud. He looked lost and confused.

'Mum, I'm really sorry,' he whispered.

'What are you sorry for, babe?' I had to blink away the tears.

'I think I broke my glasses,' he said, holding out the mangled frames.

It was too painful to watch.

'Don't be silly, they can be replaced.' I kissed him, tears rolling down my cheeks.

I clasped my hand nervously over my mouth as I watched Daniel being lifted onto a stretcher.

'Mummy, Mummy,' he cried as they secured his head.

'I'm right here, babe,' I promised, hovering over him.

'He's a very lucky lad,' I overheard one of the mums on the school run who had stopped to stare.

'The vehicle in front was a lorry. He would have been

dead if he'd stepped out a few seconds earlier,' she wittered to her friends.

I felt sick. So sick I was going to throw up. I stuck my fist into my mouth to stop the retching.

'Are you coming in the ambulance?' said the paramedic closing the doors of the ambulance.

'Yes,' I replied, jacking my leg up.

'Mum, I want to come with you,' Mitchell said, charging forward. One of the mums had volunteered to take care of him but Mitchell had broken free from her grip.

'It's best if you stay.' I tried to push him away.

'Please, Mum,' he quivered. His eyes were red and swollen from crying.

I signalled for him to jump in with me.

'He's going to be OK, isn't he?' Mitchell whispered as we shot through the country lanes to the hospital.

Nee naaw neee naaw. The siren sounded so different from inside the ambulance. Dan was as quiet as a mouse. I couldn't take my eyes off him – I watched his every twitch.

'What the hell happened, boy?' I asked Mitchell.

'He was running away.'

'From who?' I shrieked.

'Two lads who were chasing him. They've had it in for him for ages.' His mouth turned south in sadness.

I'd failed him again. He was being bullied and I hadn't protected him.

The ambulance screeched to a stop, the back doors were flung open and I was blinded by the sunlight streaming in.

Daniel was pulled out and wheeled through the double doors of A&E.

'Mummy!' he cried as I chased after them into the resuscitation room.

'You can't go in there,' a nurse said, stopping me as the swinging doors closed in my face. I scraped my hands through my long hair in frustration.

'Is he going to be OK, Mum?' Mitchell asked, badgering me for answers I didn't have.

I pulled out a five-pound note from my bag and handed it to my son.

'Can you get me a cup of coffee?' I smiled, knowing that by giving him a note he would have to traipse all the way to the canteen rather than use the vending machines. It bought me some time, enough time to slip through the double doors by myself.

My baby, my poor baby.

Daniel was lying helplessly while doctors flew around him. Monitors were bleeping and medics were talking in code. I couldn't find a place to stand because so many people were in there.

'Could you wait outside?' a nurse said, gently leading me back through the doors.

Dan screamed.

'Wait,' I yelped, turning on my heels and charging back through. I needed to protect him.

'Please,' the nurse said firmly, pinning me back with her hand. She had a lot of strength behind her tiny frame.

'You can watch through the window.' She pointed.

Dan was screaming as they tried to put a drip in his arm. Poor Dan, he hates needles. *Be strong, boy*. I stood on my tiptoes as I watched the drama unfold.

Eventually a doctor came out to chat to me. He pulled off his surgical mask as he led me to the side of the corridor.

'He's a very lucky boy,' he began.

'I know,' I mumbled.

'He sustained serious concussion, so we'll have to keep him in over night . . .' He then paused to catch his breath. '. . . but he's going to be OK,' he said, and smiled.

'Oh, thank God.' I covered my mouth with relief. 'Thank God, thank God.'

Tears filled my eyes.

I picked up the phone and dialled John. He gave me an earful for not calling him earlier and then said he was on his way. I stayed by Dan's bedside all night, listening to his soft breathing. Imagining how close I came to losing him.

I had just weeks to prepare for my second-year exams but I couldn't concentrate on anything for longer than five minutes. Daniel was off school and I would find myself staring at his battered and bruised body as he lay stretched across the sofa.

I can't believe he's alive. I can't believe how close I got to losing him.

Amanda and Louise did their best to pick me up but I couldn't talk about the accident without crying. They squeezed my hand as we walked into the exam room but I was already somewhere else. I was back on that roadside, looking at my son's bloodstained face.

'You have three hours and forty-five minutes to complete the first paper,' the invigilator said, walking up and down the aisle. I stared out of the window, my eyes glazing over.

I don't know how I managed to pass those exams. I ended up with one 2.1, a third and two 2.2s. It meant I would have to pull off some miracle to get a 2.1 in my final year.

I started my last year at university feeling defeated. My dream of proving to myself, to my mum, that I could pass with flying colours was slipping away. I needed someone to give me a hug. It was like Gary Briggs read my mind. A text message from him arrived after a year of silence:

Mum says you passed your exams. Well done.

I was still in touch with his mum. I clung to anyone who might become a replacement to my own mum.

I didn't pass with flying colours but thanks anyway, I replied. I pushed for some answers: Why are you texting me after all this time?

I just wanted to wish you well. I was wondering how you was doing?

We met up for a drink and I let him back into my car wreck of a life. I missed him. I was feeling low.

Within weeks of moving back in, Gary proposed. We were having an Indian at a restaurant in Brightlingsea when he got down on one knee between the courses of poppadoms and chicken korma.

'Will you marry me?' he said, his eyes twinkling with happiness. The room fell silent as everyone dropped their cutlery to stare at us.

'Get up off the floor.' I giggled.

'Will ya?' he said, beaming.

'Yeah, of course I'll marry you,' I said, and laughed.

The restaurant erupted in cheers and claps and my cheeks turned crimson with embarrassment. It was a simple proposal but very romantic. I'd always dreamt of getting married so I could be in a family. So I could be a different kind of wife and mother from my mum.

I leant across the table and kissed him on his curry-stained lips.

'I love you,' I whispered. It was a moment of happiness I could pocket for ever. That I could pull out and remember when the storm hit again.

22

Against All Odds

I would have fallen asleep if my elbow hadn't been propping my head up on the desk. We were close to our finals and I was exhausted from all the studying and panicking about how I was going to pass after messing up my second year.

I'd need to get four 2.1s in my exams to get a 2.1 overall. I needed a miracle. My eyelids started to roll down as we covered the Law of Evidence in our lecture.

I need some sleep, just two minutes rest.

'So today we are going to cover the sexual offences act in more detail because there will be an exam question on it.' The lecturer pulled down the projector screen.

'Her voice sounds so nasal, like she has a permanently blocked nose,' Mel whispered. Mel was our new recruit to our study team. She was about the same age as me and had very curly dark hair.

'Shush, I like this evidence stuff, it's like what they do on that TV show *CSI*,' said Louise, grinning.

My sleepy thoughts turned to the glossy TV series as I imagined the detectives pulling on their latex gloves and finding a spot of blood under an ultraviolet light.

'The sexual offences act is particularly important as a new act has been passed which has seen a number of differences,' the lecturer carried on. She pointed to the board with her cane.

'Number one . . .' she started.

My elbow slid along the desk as I nearly dropped off to sleep. We were now covering 'statute of limitations'.

'So is there a limit of time on bringing charges against a sexual offender?' one of the geeks on the front row asked.

'No,' replied the lecturer.

My body jolted awake. It was a feeling I'd only experienced once before – when I was sitting in my sex education class at school. The lecturer's voice faded into an echo and everyone around me vanished. It felt like I was sitting alone in the big hall, with just my thoughts and memories for company.

So I could get him done then.

Wow.

I could put my stepdad behind bars.

'Tina . . .' Amanda tried to get my attention. 'Hello, earth to Tina,' she said.

'Uh, yeah, what have I missed?' I said as I came back into my body.

'You look like you've seen a ghost.' Amanda stared at my pale face.

'Yeah, something like that.' I arched my eyebrow.

'Be quiet, you girls,' the lecturer interrupted our whispers.

I threw my thoughts back into my textbook for the remaining half an hour. I wanted to sit on my discovery until

I had room to think and breathe. Imagine finding out you could prosecute the man who ruined your life, after all. What do you do? What should you do? It would shatter my brothers. It would destroy my mum. She would hate me for ever.

I can't do it. I can't ever think about it.

I channelled my years of pent-up anger into my exams instead. I revised into the small hours and got up at the crack of dawn to start again. I wanted to prove to *them* that I could achieve something, that I could get a bloody law degree.

'OK, time's up,' the examiner said, as I desperately tried to write a few extra sentences. I buried my face into my hands, wishing I'd answered the other question.

'How did you find that?' Amanda asked as we stepped wearily into the summer sunshine.

'Oh God, I think I screwed up,' I sighed. I deserved a 2.1 from the amount of work I'd put in but the odds were heavily against me.

'Can we not talk about it,' I pleaded. I hated when everyone talks about the exam and you suddenly realise you answered the wrong question and your heart sinks. It reminded me of school. The results were going to be put online in a few weeks. I had three weeks to dream I'd got a 2.1 before reality hit.

On the day of reckoning I was sitting in the living room with my laptop on my knees, refreshing the page every few seconds.

I got a 2.2, I know I have. I messed up.

My heart was galloping as I closed in on the finishing line. I'd never wanted something so much in my life. I'd overcome the odds to make it to university and I just wanted someone to give me a break.

I want a 2.1, Please give me a 2.1.

I jumped as my mobile vibrated.

'They're up, they're up,' Mel screeched.

Oh, God. Please, God.

'Bloody hell, I got a 2.1,' she squealed. 'I can't believe it.' I could imagine her jumping around her bedroom. I was happy for her but gutted at the same time because she had what I wanted.

'What did you get?' Mel asked.

I burst into tears.

'Tina, babe, what did you get?' Mel pushed me to speak.

'I got a 2.2,' I sobbed. I knew it, I bloody knew it.

'Oh, babe,' Mel whimpered.

'Please don't be upset,' she started her pep talk. 'You've achieved so much. Every year you have had something thrown at you. Don't be disappointed that you have a 2.2.'

'But I really wanted a 2.1, I worked so hard,' I said, swallowing my tears.

The dream was over. I could hear my mum's voice in my head: 'Never mind love, you weren't clever enough to get a 2.1.' Amanda and Louise texted to say they also got 2.1s. My heart sank into my stomach. Mel kept talking but her words fell on deaf ears. I was devastated.

'What does it actually say?' Mel prodded.

'Huh?' I frowned.

'It says I have got a second-class honours and then it has "one" in brackets after it,' I read from the computer screen.

'You idiot,' Mel shrieked. 'That's a 2.1. You dopey cow.'

'Oh, my God . . .' my voice trailed off.

I jumped up and screamed. I went from being tearful to elated in a split second.

'I did it, I bloody did it.' Now tears of joy were streaming down my cheeks.

Choke on that, Mum.

I told Mel to round up the girls for celebratory drinks and then I dialled Gary and my friends. I rang every single person I knew before my mum. I wanted her to find out second-hand about my degree, I wanted her to know what it feels like to not be put first. I got my results at 2 p.m. and I dialled Mum at her office at 4.45 p.m.

'All right,' she grunted. I couldn't tell if she knew already. I hope she did.

'I got my results,' I said, beaming.

'Did you pass?'

'Yeah, I got a 2.1.'

'Oh, right, is that good then?' She couldn't have sounded less interested if she tried.

'Yeah,' I said, swallowing my anger.

'Oh, right. Anyway, I gotta go because I'm going home in a minute . . .' she trailed off.

'OK, see you later.' I shook my head with disgust. I knew it, I knew she wouldn't give a shit. I thought getting a degree and making something of myself would make her love me at last. But I should have known better. She just didn't care. I had to finally accept my mother didn't give a damn about me. The writing had been on the wall for years but I'd refused to see it.

I was given three complimentary tickets for my graduation, which I gave to my fiancé Gary and my two boys. I was so proud of how they had supported me in my final year and I wanted them by my side. Anyone else would have to pay £15. The week before the ceremony, Mum rang me up.

'So are you doing the whole thing with the gown and stuff?' she said.

'Yes,' I replied. I was waiting for it . . .

'Well, am I going to get an invite?' she barked like she couldn't believe why she didn't have one already.

'If you want to pay £15 for a ticket you are more than welcome to come,' I said calmly and businesslike.

'Why have I gotta pay £15?'

'Because the free tickets went to Gary and my children,' I explained.

'Well, I'm coming to your party you're having on the Saturday, so I'll leave it,' she said and shrugged off the most important day of my life.

Unbelievable.

'OK,' I said through gritted teeth and hung up. Gary was sitting beside me and watched my face turn red with rage.

'Are you OK?' he asked tentatively.

'No, I'm not,' I said. I'd never felt so much hatred. It was the straw that broke the camel's back. I was fed up with carrying her guilt around on my shoulders.

'That bitch won't pay £15 to see her only daughter graduate.' I flung my arms into the air. 'I'm sick to death of trying to please that woman.'

I was angrier at my mum at that very moment than I'd ever been at my stepdad. I pitied David Moore, whereas I hated my mum for letting me down, again.

I tried to blot out my disappointment on my graduation day so as not to ruin my crowning moment. I got up early and straightened my hair, which was now so long it almost reached to my bum. I liked to joke I was Samson, that my strength was in my hair, which I hadn't cut, apart from the occasional trim, since I was a teenager.

I ironed my white blouse and helped Gary do up his tie. He looked so dapper in a suit. I threw on my black gown and adjusted my hat and asked him to take a picture.

'I'm so proud of you, babe,' he said, grinning from behind the camera. He'd put the jealousy that tore us apart behind him and he was clearly so happy for me.

'Can I try your hat on?' Mitchell asked.

'Go on then,' I said, placing it on his head.

'It doesn't fit,' he said as he tried to balance it.

'You have to study as hard as me and then your brain will grow into it,' I teased.

I thought the ceremony would go on for ever but it whizzed by. I told the girls I wanted to do it all over again as we drank champagne in the marquee.

'If she hasn't sent me a message by the end of this afternoon, that's it,' I whispered into Gary's ear. He knew what I was talking about. He knew I couldn't take my mind off it. I'd been handed so many congratulations cards and even John had sent me a text that morning saying how proud he was of me. But it was creeping up to 5 p.m. and there was still no message from my mum. I sank another glass of champagne and checked my phone again.

Nothing.

I blinked away my tears, which were burning to get out.

'Are you all right?' Amanda squeezed my arm.

'Yeah.' I smiled. I was so happy but so sad at the same time. It was a paralysing feeling I'd suffered with my whole life and I couldn't do it any more. I pulled away from the group and sat on a ribbon-decorated chair in the corner.

I poured my heart out in a text message to my mum:

Mum, I am not doing this any more. I will not be second place to that man any more. How can I ever please you when I can never do enough? Don't contact me any more.

I switched off my phone and downed another glass of champagne. She'd taken enough of my thoughts.

When we got home I called the boys over for a chat. Mitchell and Dan took a seat either side of me on the green leather sofa in our lounge.

'I just want to let you know I won't be seeing your nan any more,' I said.

'Why?' Dan gasped.

'But she's our nan, I'd like to stay in touch with her,' Mitchell whined.

'That's fine but first you need to hear my story,' I went on. It was time my boys found out about my past.

'You know Nan lives with a man who you never see?'

'Yeah,' they said in chorus.

'Well, that man sexually assaulted me when I was a child.' I paused to check their reactions. Dan looked sad and Mitchell's eyes looked angry.

'And Mum is still living with this man, knowing he has done that to me.'

'I can't believe she would do that to you. I don't want nothing more to do with her either,' Mitchell snapped.

'Me too,' Dan mumbled.

'Are you OK, Mum,' Dan asked, with tears in his eyes.

'Yeah, I'm fine, I have you to protect me.' I pulled them in for a cuddle.

I must have drunk more than I realised that night as I woke the next morning with bleary eyes and a stinking hangover. I rolled across the bed to reach for a glass of water. My phone was resting on the side table, teasing me to switch it back on. I had to know what she'd replied. If she'd replied at all.

I don't think that's very fair I do love you, bleeped through her message.

Lies, all lies, I thought. *If you loved me you would have protected me from that monster.*

I tapped the words: That's enough. I don't ever want to hear from you again.

I pressed SEND.

I fell back onto my pillow with a surge of relief. It had taken twenty years but she was finally out of my life.

Finally I was free from my past.

23

A Weight Is Lifted

My boys were right, I had suffocated them.

I hadn't allowed them much freedom because I was frightened of someone getting to them. They were now thirteen and fourteen but I still stopped them going out after dark. I would take them along with me if I went out in the evenings. But after what happened to me you can understand why, can't you? I was terrified of someone abusing my boys. I'd promised to protect them.

'Tina, can I get you anything?' Gary tried to get me to speak.

'No, leave me alone,' I whispered, clutching my pillow like it was a baby. My boys had left me and I felt like someone had ripped out my heart.

They were only meant to go to John's for the weekend but they never came back. They had told John that they were fed up with not having any freedom and their dad had promised to give them everything I had denied them. John always said he would get his own back for taking his kids away from him and running off to a refuge. Well, he got his revenge. He had destroyed me.

Every time I moved I wanted to be sick with unhappiness. I couldn't eat, my stomach was so knotted. All I wanted to think about was how overprotective I had been – torturing myself by replaying every memory. Only a few months had passed since graduating – I should have still been celebrating, not wishing I was dead.

I sent Mitchell and Dan another text message: I know you're angry with me, but I'm here if you need me.

I hurled my phone across the room in anger.

'Tina, they are just being teenagers. You are a great mum,' Gary tried to reassure me. He sat by my side and stroked my hair.

'You don't understand.' I shook my head free. 'You don't know why I am the way I am.'

Gary stared at me blankly.

'I, I . . .' I couldn't get the words out.

'What, babe?' Gary stroked me.

I pulled away from him so I could put my armour on.

'I was raped by my stepdad,' I spluttered. I wrapped my hands around the back of my head and buried my face into my arms. I couldn't look at Gary. 'I lost my virginity to him.'

'It went on for a long time.'

I broke down sobbing.

Silence.

Say something, please say something.

'Why the fuck have you never told me this before?' he said, backing off.

No, don't leave me.

'I'm sorry. When was there ever a good time to tell you this?' I snapped like a cornered dog.

He shook his head. I was losing him.

'I'd been desperate to tell you but there was never a right time,' I cried.

Hug me, please just hug me.

Gary clearly couldn't understand. He walked outside and lit a cigarette, leaving me feeling dirty and rejected. I was on the cusp of losing everyone who I loved. Gary walked back in, smelling of smoke, and frowned at me.

'I'm so sorry I reacted like that; it was too much to take in.' He smiled sadly.

'You didn't need to know before. It was part of my past. And it wasn't a happy past,' I said, shaking with fear of being alone.

He knelt beside me and pulled me into his chest with his long skinny arms. He kissed my forehead and told me how sorry he was for me, that he loved me and he would be there for me. I cried until I ran out of tears.

I went downhill from there. As the weeks rolled past without any word from my kids I slipped into depression. I couldn't sleep and would stay up all night doing puzzles, which I'd ordered off eBay. I'd doze on the sofa during the day, checking my phone repeatedly to see if the boys had texted me. The housework went out the window. I didn't even want to wash myself. Gary tried to pick me up but he had no idea what it felt like as a mother to lose your children – it was like losing a part of my body.

I wanted to die. I wanted someone to set me free so I could finally be at peace.

Another week passed in a blur and I was now having anxiety attacks where my heart would beat too fast for my body. I was curled up on our big brown sofa one night, staring into our vile blue carpet, when it hit me like a dart.

'It's all your fault,' I mumbled like a madwoman.

The reason I was overprotective of my kids was because of my stepdad. I would have allowed them to breathe and do all the things they should have done at their age if David Moore hadn't raped me.

I'd had enough.

I'm going to get the man who started all of this.

And I know I can, thanks to my law degree.

'I'm going to ring the police and tell them what my stepdad did,' I announced to Gary.

His mouth dropped. 'Are you sure?'

'He deserves to pay. He took my childhood away. I've tried to live a normal life for all these years but I can't.'

I rose to my feet in anger.

'And as for my mum, I have nothing to prove to her any more, because I've proved to myself I'm clever enough to go to university, I'm clever enough to get a good degree and I'm determined enough to achieve whatever I want to achieve in my life . . . I'm ready to go to the police.'

'I'll support you if that's what you want to do,' said Gary proudly.

I couldn't get any lower than I was then and if I did fall apart it didn't matter because I didn't have my boys to look after. It was now or never. I picked up the phone and rang Romford Police Station.

For the first time my heart wasn't racing, I was as calm as the sea on a summer's day, because I had waited twenty years to make this call. I had always been so frightened of losing my mum and my brothers but now they were gone from my life I had nothing to lose.

'I want to report a sexual abuse from my childhood,' I said to the police officer.

They took my details and said someone would be in touch. I hung up feeling strangely excited. I calmly walked upstairs, got dressed and then jumped in my car. I was just about to hit the M25 when an unknown number flashed across the screen of my mobile phone.

'Is that Tina Renton?'

My heart stopped as I knew who it was. Suddenly it became real and I was scared.

'Yes,' I replied, pulling over.

'You reported a case of sexual abuse,' confirmed the police officer.

'That's right.' I took a deep breath.

I arranged to make a statement the next day. It was all moving so fast my feet were no longer touching the ground. I was scared but I didn't regret it for a second.

It was a dreary cold day when I turned up at Chadwell Heath Police Station wearing a cardigan and jeans in November 2009. I hugged my body to keep warm as I pressed the buzzer on the iron-clad gates.

'Tina Renton to see Julia Godfrey,' I spoke into the crackle. The gates opened and I walked through. I'd chosen to make my statement alone because I didn't want to have to put on a brave face in front of someone I loved. I'd never spoken about the details of what my stepfather did to me –

not to my best friend or to my husband-to-be. I was terrified about opening Pandora's box but I was also determined.

There was no going back.

Julia met me at the door, with a big warm smile and a handshake. I'd imagined the police station to look like something out of the TV series *The Bill*, with officers walking around in uniform and walkie-talkies blaring. But everyone was in civvies because they were working undercover for the child abuse unit. I wouldn't have known they were cops.

Julia led me into a tiny room that smelt of instant noodles and coffee. The walls were dirty while the window looked like it was going to fall out at any moment and the blinds were hanging on by a thread. In the centre was a desk with just a box of tissues on top.

Julia signalled for me to take a seat in the worn armchair.

'Would you like a cup of tea?' she asked.

I nodded. The blinds rattled as she shut the door and I was left with my thoughts.

What if she doesn't believe me? What if she thinks it was my fault? If I hadn't taken that money my stepfather left on my bedside, maybe he wouldn't have raped me?

Julia broke into my spiralling thoughts just in time. She pushed my cup across the table and I hugged its warmth with both hands.

'Are you ready?' She smiled.

'Ready as I'll ever be.' I sighed deeply.

She shuffled her papers and then poised her pen ready to take my statement.

'OK, we'll start from the beginning. When did David Moore first come into your life?'

I cast my mind back to when I lived in Maygreen Crescent. I told Julia how at first David seemed like the dad I'd never had. How he looked after me while my mum sat on her arse watching TV downstairs.

'I didn't know any better when he started drying me with the towel,' I recounted. 'I thought that's what all dads did with their daughters.'

Julia would frown and look sorry for me but I kept my composure. I'd gained so much confidence through university that I felt like I had found the strength of a knight. I sat tall and proud in that interview room, approaching every question clinically like a doctor in an operating theatre.

Julia's hand must have been aching with the amount of detail she was delving into.

'In what position were you lying on your bed when he raped you?' she asked.

'On my side,' I replied.

She pushed over a piece of paper and asked me to draw the layout of my bedroom. All she wanted was facts, which made the process much easier to stomach because I didn't have to attach any emotion to what I was describing.

'Can I have another cup of tea?' I asked for my eighth cup.

'Would you like a break?' Julia smiled.

'No, I want to keep going.'

I had so much to tell that we had to stagger it over three

days in the end. I never cried once – until I spoke about my mum.

'Why are you coming forward now?' Julia asked.

I was emotionally exhausted. My eyes were stinging from concentrating so hard. I sighed deeply and explained:

'It's down to my mum really . . . I've tried to please her my whole life so I couldn't go to the police. That would have been the ultimate betrayal.'

Don't cry, don't cry tears over her.

'I was fighting every day to give her what she wanted.'

The tears started to well.

'But when I made that decision to cut her out of my life, I didn't have to worry about how it would affect her or my brothers any more.'

I dabbed the corners of my eyes but it was too late, I couldn't stop them.

'It was the right time.' I took a deep breath.

'I'm not trying to please her any more.' Another deep breath.

'I've got nothing to prove to her any more. I'm no longer living a lie.' A single tear ran down my cheek.

Julia stroked my hand and passed me a tissue.

'I'm sorry,' I blubbered.

'Sorry for what?' Julia frowned.

'I dunno, for getting emotional.'

'You are a very strong, brave woman,' she said, and smiled.

'There is another reason why I am here today. Both my brothers are now in relationships and I swore if either of them went on to have children I would never put another little girl in jeopardy.'

Breathe, Tina, breathe.

'He deserves to pay for what he did to me,' I said, sinking my head into my hands.

I took a slurp of tea and fell back into my chair with relief.

'And it's also about confidence.' I'd found my fighter voice again.

'How do you mean?' Julia asked, furrowing her brow.

'Getting my degree has given me a massive amount of confidence. I've never really had any confidence but achieving that was amazing.' I sighed reflectively. 'It has made me realise if you want something bad enough, if you try, you can succeed.'

Julia nodded proudly.

'Are you glad it's over?' Julia asked as she pointed to where I had to sign the statement.

'Yeah, I feel like you believe me,' I said.

'Of course I believe you. I have no reason to doubt you. We now need to build a case.'

Julia explained that because it was a historical inquiry, that there was no physical evidence, it was essentially my word against his, so she would need to build up a case by speaking to as many witnesses as possible. It would then be handed to the Crown Prosecution Service who would decide whether to take it further.

'Will he be arrested?' I imagined David's face as he was cuffed.

'It's a bit early to tell,' she replied. I could tell Julia was being careful not to give me false hope.

'But you have given an excellent statement and will make a brilliant witness,' she added.

I felt like a weight had been lifted off my shoulders as I walked out of the police station.

There, I've done my bit, now get the bastard.

I couldn't cope with thinking about the next stage. The arrest. A trial. Standing up and telling the world what he did to me. At least I didn't need to worry about David, my mum or my brothers getting at me because none of them knew where I lived. We'd recently moved to Rainham – I was still in Brightlingsea for all they knew.

It was evening by the time I drove home and I became stuck in High Street traffic.

'Come on, move,' I yelled at the car in front. 'MOVE!' I screamed.

And just like that, my armour shattered to the car floor. I burst into tears as the stress of the past three days exploded out of me. I was also still grieving the loss of my boys. Gary was waiting for me with a hug as I walked through the front door.

'How did it go?' he asked tentatively.

'Yeah, OK.' I slung my handbag to the ground and fell onto our big snuggly brown sofa.

'Was it really hard because it brought back all those bad memories?'

I sighed deeply and beckoned him over to the sofa.

'It didn't bring back memories because they have always been there. I've just learnt to live with them for over twenty years.'

He looked at me blankly. He didn't know how to comfort me.

'I'm so glad I've done it though,' I went on. 'I want him to go to jail, even if it's just for six months. I want him to pay for what he did to me.

'And I want my brothers, my mum, their friends, I want everyone who may have judged my behaviour along the way, to know exactly what he did to me. I want people to know there was a reason why I acted the way I did over the years,' I said, the lawyer in me coming out.

'He picked the wrong person to mess with,' Gary said, and smiled.

'Damn right he did.'

24

The Big Day

'Don't cry, don't cry,' I whispered to Gary. 'Or you'll start me off.'

I let out a nervous giggle as everyone's eyes were watching us at the altar. Gary gave me a loving smile and I blinked away the tears – I couldn't ruin my make-up, not before the wedding photos.

I looked up into his blue eyes and my stomach somersaulted. Gary looked gorgeous in his cream waistcoat, red tie and black wedding jacket. He had a glowing tan and his hair was neatly cropped short.

'I love you,' I mouthed before we turned to face the vicar.

The chitter chatter behind us hushed silent as the vicar began the ceremony.

'We have come here today ...' he started. My tummy somersaulted with happiness again. I looped my fingers through Gary's and gave them a gentle loving squeeze.

It was 11 June 2010, and the sun was pouring down on us through the church windows like a spotlight. The hall smelt deliciously of flowers and perfumes. We paused to sing another hymn and then the vicar said something I'll never forget.

'Marriage is like having a rucksack full of rocks on your back,' he started. His voice was soothing like a menthol sweet.

'Sometimes you'll give your partner more rocks, because you need help carrying your weight. Marriage is about sharing and being there for each other.'

He was right. I felt stronger knowing I would have Gary to protect and support me if my case against my stepdad went to trial. We were a team, a family.

Mitchell stepped forward with our rings twinkling on a velvet cushion. My boys looked so dapper in their suits and burgundy waistcoats. They were still living with John but at least we were speaking again.

The vicar cleared his throat. 'Repeat after me ...' he began the vows with Gary. My heart was galloping as it was my turn next.

'I, Tina Renton, take you, Gary Briggs, to be my husband.' My eyes welled with tears.

'I promise to have and to hold from this day forward, for better, for worse, for richer, for poorer, in sickness and in health until death us do part.' I bit my lip but it was too late, tears trickled down my cheeks. I was so happy.

'You may kiss the bride,' the vicar said.

We were showered with a storm of red and white confetti as we walked out of the church in Rainham to greet our friends and Gary's family.

If my mum could see me now.

I hadn't heard from her since I sent her that text and I was glad she wasn't there for my wedding. She would have soured my big day. The only three members of my family I'd invited were the ones who barely spoke to my mum – her sister, Gayna, and her mum, my nan, Iris, and grandad, Stanley. I hoped the news would filter back to her and she'd choke on it. I wanted her to know what she'd missed.

'Come here, you two.' I beckoned Mitchell and Dan over for a picture. They were my ushers and they looked so grown up.

'You've done such a brilliant job, I'm so proud of you both.' I hugged and kissed them.

'Muuuum,' Dan cringed, wiping his cheek.

'Can't your mum give you a kiss?' I teased.

Things were gradually getting better between us. I was now seeing the boys once every couple of weeks. I was glad they weren't living with me as I'd been given the heads up by Julia Godfrey that she hadn't spoken to my mum or brothers yet, but the investigation was taking shape and I didn't want my boys to see me if I fell apart. I'd protected them up until now but I'd have to let them know if the cat was going to be let out of the bag. I just had to choose the right moment.

'Another picture of the lovely bride and groom . . .' The photographer squeezed me and Gary together.

'Are you happy?' he whispered in my ear.

'I'm so happy,' I said and kissed him.

'Ahhh, lovely shot . . .' said the photographer, capturing the moment.

Gary whisked me away to Mexico for our honeymoon and I plodded on as normal when we got back. I was working for an insurance company just to bring some money in while I tried to secure a training contract in a law firm. I put the police investigation to the back of my mind just like I had to do when I was kid – it was my coping mechanism.

I was driving to the office on 8 July when I noticed a missed call on my mobile phone.

Julia Godfrey the child protection officer and she's left a voice-mail.

'Can you give me a ring, I need to ask you something?' she said after the bleep.

I pulled over immediately and dialled her back. I had a terrible feeling something was up.

'Hi, Tina,' she answered on the second ring.

'We've executed a warrant at your mum's home,' she said, dropping the bombshell. 'We are here now.'

Oh, my God, oh, *my God*.

'Your mum is not happy,' she added.

I imagined my mum f'ing and blinding on her doorstep in her dressing gown with a fag hanging out of her angry mouth.

'Oh, right,' I replied. Suddenly I felt scared. I hadn't seen this coming. I wish Julia had warned me. It had all become very real.

'Is David there?' I asked tentatively.

'He is at work. I've just taken a statement from your mum saying it's the first she has ever heard of such an allegation.

'Liar,' I spat. And then I started laughing. *Liar liar liar.*

'I'm ringing because we want to find the teddy bear your stepdad asked you to touch yourself with.

'Oh, OK.' I was still in shock.

'What did it look like?' she probed.

'It was a brown bear.'

'How big was it?'

'Umm, normal size. I guess it seemed much bigger to me when I was little.' I shrugged.

'We'll check the loft. Keep your phone on, I'll call you later,' Julia rang off.

I was left feeling like I'd been punched in the stomach. I couldn't get the vision of my mum's screwed-up angry face out of my head as I sat behind my desk at work. The cat had finally been let out of the bag, and I was scared what would happen next. I wasn't regretting what I had done but I couldn't help feeling I'd betrayed my mum. I'd screwed her over. You can't undo years of wanting to please someone, just like that. And on the flip side of the coin I was excited that they were finally going to answer for how they made me suffer. I was smiling and welling up with tears at the same time. I sat on my hands until lunch and then I rang Julia again. I had to know what was going on.

'We have left your mum's home now, and we've made arrangements for David Moore to be questioned at the police station on Monday at 10 a.m. Are you OK?' she softened. It must be hard to do her job, be tough all the time.

'Yeah, just upset my mum lied about how I told her the truth all those years ago,' I said. 'But I should have expected that.'

'Keep it together for the weekend and we'll speak on Monday,' Julia encouraged.

I tried to push it to the back of my mind but it was getting harder. I'd be doing the shopping and then my mum's voice would tunnel into my head. 'That ungrateful bitch, I can't believe she's done this to us.' I could imagine her throwing things around the room in fury while Dave sat quietly, pathetically.

'I bet she's told Blake and Jonathan I made the whole thing up. I bet she is calling me every name under the sun,' I said to Gary.

'Let her, that's not for you to worry about now,' Gary said, trying to calm me down.

Julia Godfrey rang me on Monday evening: 'We've interviewed David Moore and he has denied everything.'

I burst out laughing. 'No surprise there then.' I shook my head in disgust. David was bailed to reappear at the police station in September but no charges had been made against him.

The summer came and went. David was bailed again to reappear in late December. The autumn came and went. None of my family tried to contact me, thank God. Winter arrived and Julia Godfrey called me.

'You can't tell anyone this at the moment,' she said, sounding breathless.

'I promise,' I said. It was so cold I could see my own breath as I clutched the phone.

'David Moore will be charged tomorrow,' she revealed.

Pause. She'd taken my breath away.

'Really?' I finally spoke, arching my eyebrow.

'Yes, really. When he comes in tomorrow to answer bail

again, we will charge him. The CPS feels confident that it is a case and that you will make an excellent witness.'

I smiled to myself.

And I felt relief. Even though I knew it was going to get worse before it got better, I was relieved because I was believed. I'd had to live a lie with my family for so long that I was terrified people would think I'd made it up. Julia's words gave me the boost of confidence I'd been searching for.

I'd been getting on much better with John for the past few months and since Gary was working all hours under the sun I asked my ex if he would come to Romford Police Station with me on the morning of 18 December.

'David Moore is answering bail again and I just want to see his face when he leaves the police station,' I lied.

What I really wanted to do was see the fear on my step-dad's face when he is told he's being charged. Finally he gets to know what it feels like to be scared and I didn't want to miss that moment for the world. I couldn't tell John that though because I'd promised Julia I'd keep my mouth shut.

John was only too happy to be my accomplice. The last time he'd seen David Moore was cowering behind my mum when he'd gone around their house to tell her how he had tried to rape me, again.

He brought his sister Julie along, and the three of us sat in his BMW X5 in the garage next to the police station. It was a boy-racer's car and conveniently had blacked-out windows. We had the heater blasting to keep us warm on that chilly winter morning.

I was sitting in the back, leaning forward with my arms

wrapped around both headrests. We watched the entrance like we were some undercover surveillance team. The hours crept past and lots of jokes and instant coffees from the garage later, my phone rang. It was a withheld number.

'That's a copper, that's Julia.' I looked at it like it would explode.

'Well fucking answer it then,' John yelped. We were on the edge of our seats with excitement.

'Are you OK?' came Julia's familiar voice.

'Yeah.'

'Are you on your own?' she asked.

I'm watching the police station right as we speak, waiting for the bastard to leave.

'No, I'm with John and his sister,' I said, telling her a half-truth.

'OK, he's been charged with thirteen offences.'

I was speechless.

'He has to appear at Romford Magistrates Court on the 23rd of December,' she went on.

'Thanks for letting me know,' I said and then hung up. I was so in shock I forgot to ask her what the charges were.

John stared at me, trying to gauge my reaction.

'Well?'

'He's been charged with thirteen offences.' I shook my head in disbelief.

A Cheshire cat grin spread across John's face. Without saying anything he got out of the car, licked his finger, and wrote a massive thirteen in the dirt on his bonnet. Julie and I sniggered like naughty schoolchildren.

'He can see it in writing when he comes out,' John scoffed.

We waited another twenty minutes but John had to go to work.

'Let's go,' I said. 'I don't need to see him now he's been charged.'

'Are you sure?'

'Yep, let's go.'

As we were driving back, Julie and John were chatting away about how much David Moore deserved to pay but I was sat in the back wrapped up in my own world. *What's going to happen now? How did he take the news? What's Mum saying? How are my brothers taking the news? Thirteen, where did they get thirteen from?*

I wound down the window and took in a deep gulp of icy air.

Is he scared? I hope he's so terrified he can't sleep at night.

25

What Doesn't Kill You Makes You Stronger

'I can't do this any more,' Gary announced while we were eating a curry.

'It's over.'

His words hit me like a ten-tonne truck that I hadn't seen coming.

'Why?' I burst out crying.

Why will no one love me? What's wrong with me? Don't leave me to fight this alone.

'I can't cope with the trial,' he said coldly.

'How are you not coping with the trial? You're not the one going through it?' I screamed over the table. 'I told you not to come. You're not going to be there when I give evidence. What have you got to cope with?' I jabbed my finger at him.

I pushed my plate away, the smell was making me want to be sick.

'We've only been married seven months,' I said in disbelief.

He looked at me with guilty eyes.

'I've had enough, I just can't do it any more,' he said, and shook his head.

Our relationship had been rocky for the past few months. I'd been preoccupied with the trial, which had been set for 27 June 2011 after my stepdad pleaded 'Not guilty'. And Gary had been married to his job rather than me. He was working all hours, getting up at 5.30 a.m., back at 7.30 p.m., then straight to bed. He'd even worked on Christmas Day.

'I've been doing my best to shield you from everything that's been going on,' I snapped. 'And this is how you repay me.'

I wanted to throw my plate at him. Instead, I picked up my phone and called his mum in desperation.

'Your son has decided after seven months to end our marriage,' I cried down the phone to his mum, Chris.

'Calm down, Tina,' she said, trying to hush my sobs.

'I can't calm down, Gary wants to end our marriage.' I was distraught.

'What on earth for?'

'I don't know. You speak to him,' I spluttered, pressing the phone into my husband's hand.

Gary gave me a look to say 'Thanks a lot' and then took himself off into our bedroom. I could still hear every word though.

'I just can't do this any more. I don't love her any more,' he told her.

I grabbed my car keys and ran out the front door. I couldn't sit there and listen to how much he didn't love me, because it was ripping me in half. I drove to John's sister Julie's house, and she took me in from the cold.

'How can he leave me now, just before the trial?' I mumbled over and over like it wasn't real.

Julie handed me a cup of tea and wrapped a blanket over my shoulders as I was shivering with distress.

'He didn't have to go through the trial,' I rambled on. 'I told him I didn't want him in that courtroom when I gave evidence.'

Julie gave me a puzzled expression.

'Because I've tried my whole life to have a normal sex life. If Gary listened to what I'd been through it would ruin that part of our relationship.

'That must have been hard for him to hear. How did he take that?' Julie asked.

I sighed deeply. 'I think he found that hard to understand. But it was about survival. I had to push him away to keep him close. Can you understand that?' I dropped my head into my hands.

The two people I'd asked to go with me to court I'd chosen for a reason.

'I'm taking your brother's former friend Mark White because he's known me for sixteen years. I don't have to put on an act in front of him. And I've asked my old babysitter, Jemma, for the reason that we live far apart – I won't have to see her every day and know she has heard my most intimate secrets.'

I kicked Julie's coffee table in anger.

'I've fucking had enough!' I shouted. 'I'm sick of people

screwing me over. I'm going to finish what I've started, even if I have to do it alone.'

Triumphantly, I said, 'I'm going to get justice.'

After staying with Julie for a few days, I started to suffer with shoulder pain. It got so bad that I was admitted into hospital. Just four days after losing my husband, I was losing all feeling in the left side of my body. The doctors discovered I had a severe prolapse in my neck and I needed emergency surgery. I thought I would wake up alone from theatre and I was terrified. However, my sons were both there and waited all day for me.

I felt so alone that night after the operation. I didn't know if I would recover the feeling in my left side, but I had to find the strength from somewhere to pull through. By the time I got out of hospital, and still feeling bruised from surgery, my husband had informed the landlord that I was jobless and wouldn't be paying the rent. The £10,000 loan I got to clear his debts two weeks before he left was pretty much spent, and I had no job. He had known I was unhappy at work and he'd promised to support me while I found another job, so I'd already handed in my notice the week before he announced he was leaving.

No money, no job, almost no home, and £35,000 worth of debts that were all in my name, including the wedding paid for on my credit card. It was four months until the trial that would affect the rest of my life, regardless of the end result, and I didn't know if I could cope. I needed to be a fighter now more than I had ever been, but it was so hard. I almost gave up because I just couldn't battle anymore; I had run out of strength.

The one person I thought I could trust, the one person I let into my heart, the one person I thought who would be there for me, had left me without a fight. How could I ever trust another person after I had been hurt so badly by the man I loved?

I guess everyone has a reason why they do what they do, and this was no different. But who was going to fight for *me*? The reality was I knew I had come too far to let all the people who had stamped all over me to stop me now, so I would fight it alone.

Those weeks before the trial weren't easy. I treated every day as a new day, which was one day closer to standing up in court, but it didn't take the loneliness away. There was a big Gary-shaped hole missing in my heart and if I hadn't had the trial to fixate on I would have fallen to pieces.

I turned to my aunt Gayna for support because she was the only family I had left. I was scrabbling for any port in a storm because not only had I lost Gary, but my nan and grandad also told me they wanted to be left out of it, that they couldn't cope with being forced to choose between me and Mum. At least Gayna was on my side – she'd fallen out with my mum fifteen years ago and was disgusted when she heard how her sister had covered up for David Moore.

'I'm sorry,' Gayna said over a beer at Rainham Working Men's Club.

She was a no-nonsense kind of woman. She was similar to my mum in terms of always wearing the same clothes come rain or shine – three-quarter-length trousers, a T-shirt and sandals – but she didn't look anything like her. She had shoulder-length red frizzy hair and she wore glasses when no one was looking.

'What are you sorry for?' I asked.

'I should have done something.' She glugged a mouthful from the bottle.

'How could you do something you knew nothing about?' I felt myself start to cry.

'Don't cry,' Gayna ordered, trying to stop the water-works. Like so many of us, Gayna didn't know how to deal with people who cried. She offered me an escape though, and in those last two weeks that was exactly what I needed.

I threw on my armour and put on a brave face. Anyone who told me to prepare myself for the chance that my stepdad might get off scot-free, I disregarded. I wanted justice so badly I couldn't even consider what it would feel like not to get it. I felt touched that I had a small army to back me up through the trial. Gayna, our old neighbour, Tony Morgan, my ex, John, would all be speaking in court on my behalf and Julia Godfrey had managed to track down my old teacher Mrs Walsh and my schoolfriend Sam Aitken.

I eventually told my boys that I was taking my stepfather to court. I couldn't protect them from the truth for ever.

'We want to go with you, Mum,' Mitchell insisted. My boys had grown into young men who now wanted to protect me. I'd only told them the skeletal details of what happened to me, on my graduation day, but that was enough.

'No, babe, I don't want you hearing about the trauma I went through,' I said.

'We want to see him and watch him pay for what he did to you,' Mitchell said angrily.

'I'll think about you both when I'm in there.' I was touched by their love.

I turned to a cocktail of anxiety pills and sleeping tablets to get me through those last few days before the trial. My nightmares had become traumatic. Always the same dream – that I was trapped but no matter how loud I'd scream no one would help me. One night I was stuck in a prison with no doors or windows but I still couldn't get out. The worst dream was the cave though. It was dark and wet and all I had to see with was a tiny spotlight squeezing through a crack fifty feet above. There were lots of underwater tunnels teasing me as escape routes but I'd always run out of air and have to turn back. Were my dreams telling me to turn back? To walk away from the trial?

I'm not bloody giving up now.

26

Judgement Day

I woke up at the crack of dawn and threw on my armour for one last time.

I wore a trouser suit, white blouse and heels, which hurt like hell, but I wanted to make a good impression.

My friends Mark and Jemma acted like my bodyguards, flanking me on either side as we walked up the steps to the dingy-looking crown court in Southend. We had arrived an hour early so there would be no run-ins with my family. I hadn't heard a peep out of them but I knew my brothers wouldn't be able to hold back if they saw me.

Thanks to my law degree I knew what to expect. I knew what a courtroom looked like, I knew where the jury sat and, most importantly, I knew where I would stand to give my evidence. It didn't stop me being nervous though, and I got my first butterflies as we led through to a room at the back of the court.

How should I act? How should I stand? Should I be myself or well spoken? If I don't get upset will the jury think I'm lying?

'Hi, Tina, how are you feeling?' came Julia Godfrey's familiar voice.

'Terrified.' I laughed nervously.

The room was lounge-like with comfy chairs and a TV in the corner that was showing *Teletubbies* on mute. I looked at Jemma and she flashed me a 'be brave' smile. She was the perfect friend to have there, Jemma could say nothing but I'd still feel supported by her.

Julia pushed my statement across a coffee table to me.

'Can you read it through, make sure everything is clear in your head.'

Whoosh. The first shot of adrenalin kicked in.

'Yeah, although I'm word perfect,' I said. Even though I'd made that statement eighteen months ago, you don't forget memories like that.

The door opened and a small dark-skinned man wearing a suit and round glasses walked in.

'Tina Renton?' He held out his hand to shake.

'Yes,' I replied hesitantly.

'My name is Mr Shroff, I've been assigned by the CPS to be your barrister for the prosecution,' he said, and smiled. He was well spoken but he didn't have that icy edge I normally associated with snooty barristers. I liked him.

Mr Shroff told me he would walk me through my statement so the jury would get the full picture of what I had suffered at the hands of my stepfather. He said that Mum, my brothers, Blake's girlfriend, Sue, would all be giving evidence.

'And David?'

'Yes, David Moore will also take the stand,' he explained.

I felt sick.

'He's being tried for seventeen counts of rape and sexual assault,' he announced.

'Seventeen, it's gone up to seventeen?' I gasped.

'This is a serious case of child abuse,' he said.

I wanted to be sick.

'Tina, there is one question I need to ask you,' Mr Shroff started. I arched my eyebrow as if to say yes.

'Have you claimed for criminal compensation for what happened to you as a child?'

'No, I haven't. I have no intention to, I'm not going to and I don't want to,' I fired back. My goal was never to make money out of this, I wanted *him* to pay.

'OK, that's clear,' he chuckled.

'Blimey, you don't beat around the bush,' Mark said, and burst out laughing, melting the tension in the room.

'Tina Renton to court number two,' the Tannoy blared.

Oh, my God, I'm not ready, wait a minute.

I could feel my heart in my mouth as I looked at everyone in the room for help.

'You can do this, Tina,' Mark egged me on.

'Go get the bastard.'

I was terrified as I was led through a maze of corridors by a lady from the witness-protection team. I tottered on my heels through the main entrance, down a long corridor, up two flights of stairs, through the double doors into the court-room. Just as I was taking it all in, the court usher directed us into another small room.

'For fuck's sake,' I muttered under my breath. I didn't mean to be angry but I was nearly hyperventilating preparing myself, and now I was back in another holding pen. I felt like a racehorse waiting for the starting gun.

The new room was tiny and smelt musty of old leather and dust. The witness-protection woman tried to make small talk to calm my raging nerves.

'Looks like it's going to be a sunny day today,' she wittered.

Shut up, shut up.

I watched the second hand on the clock tick. The ticking noise was like a hammer in my head. Finally the door swung open and the court usher appeared. A tiny woman with her hair neatly swept back into a bun.

'Are you ready?' she asked. I could see the empathy in her eyes and it gave me the pick-me-up I needed.

'Not really, but I guess I have to be,' I joked.

A hushed silence fell over the big courtroom as I walked in and moved to the witness stand. I had a special screen to protect me from the gaze of David Moore. Only the judge, the jury and the legal team could see me, but I still felt like someone had stuck my face on a billboard in the centre of London – *look at me, everyone*. The jury were already seated opposite but I was too frightened to look at them

People do judge a book by a cover. I wonder how many of them are looking at me and have already decided I'm lying? I wonder how many of them are looking at me and then looking at him and thinking 'He's guilty', before I've even opened my mouth?

I glanced across to the judge and he smiled at me with his eyes as if to say I was going to be OK. It didn't stop my legs turning to jelly and I grabbed hold of the five-inch-wide shelf that ran around the inside of the box, to steady myself.

Where's the chair? How on earth am I going to stand up in these shoes all day?

Beads of sweat were running down my back and I felt so claustrophobic my suit jacket seemed like a straitjacket. Thank God none of my family was in the gallery; they weren't allowed to watch until they had given evidence. Thank God for the screen so I couldn't see my stepdad's face. I could feel him in the room though. I could almost smell his Old Spice aftershave.

I took my oath to swear the truth by Almighty God and then I had a minute to compose myself before my lawyer took to the floor. Mr Shroff cleared his throat and walked over to me.

'Can you just give the court your full name, please?'

'Tina Janet Renton.'

'How old are you, Miss Renton?'

'Thirty-six,' I said, lifting my head so the jury could see me. *God, it had been thirty years since he first laid a hand on me.*

Mr Shroff took a step back and then went straight for the throat, asking me how the abuse first started. I suddenly felt hit by a landslide of pressure to not screw up. I had one shot, one chance to get justice, and I couldn't let my nerves get the better of me.

'I'm going to ask you to be a bit more specific as to where the defendant dried you with the towel,' Mr Shroff probed for my early memories.

'Erm.' I squirmed with embarrassment. 'He would start with my shoulders and then work his way down with the towel.'

My eyes started to well up.

'He would put the towel in between my legs to dry my private area,' I went on.

'And then what would he do?' my barrister asked softly.

A single tear as hot as acid rolled down my face.

'He would use his finger to touch me around my vagina,' I said, cringing.

I'd only ever spoken about the fine detail of what my step-father did to me with Julia, and now there I was, telling the most intimate private things of my life to a room full of strangers. I felt dirty. Ashamed. Humiliated.

I scratched away the tears with my jacket sleeve because I knew it was going to get much worse.

'You said the defendant used to rub you with your teddy bear,' Mr Shroff told the jury. My cheeks burnt red with embarrassment.

'With its foot,' I mumbled.

'With its foot!' he exclaimed. 'And where would he rub?'

This is so humiliating. I want to die.

I focused on a black smudge on the wall behind the jury because I was too ashamed to look them in the eye.

'On my vagina,' I said. The tears started to stream.

'Whilst he was rubbing you with the teddy bear, what was he saying to you?'

'Predominantly nothing.' I paused as the words I really wanted to say had got stuck in my throat.

'He did on a couple of occasions say that I should rub myself with it because I'd enjoy it.' I broke down.

'Miss Renton, would you like a moment?' the judge asked.

'Can I please take off my jacket?' I whimpered.

'Of course, dear,' he said, and smiled. I was dripping with sweat and crying puddles of tears.

I took a sip of water and steadied myself on the shelf inside the box. It had become my crutch to keep me standing.

Come on, Tina, hang in there.

I fought off the next round of questions, and then the next, and then Mr Shroff brought up the subject of my mother. Suddenly I stopped thinking about my stepdad behind that screen, about impressing the jury, as I knew I was going to have to use up every last ounce of courage to get through this round.

'What conversation was there between you and your mother after you told her what had been happening?' asked Mr Shroff.

It was 12.40 p.m. when Mr Shroff asked me that question. The time is imprinted in my mind.

'She told me she believed me,' I said, the words feeling heavy on my tongue. 'But she was also concerned that we would lose the house, that without him being in the house we wouldn't be able to pay the mortgage. She said it was up to me but, if he came back, it would be purely for financial reasons. And she would put a lock on my bedroom door,' I choked.

'How did you feel about being told this?' Mr Shroff looked concerned.

For a moment I couldn't speak.

'I was upset because I didn't want to be responsible for putting everyone on the streets,' I said, forcing the words out. 'Because I felt it was my fault.'

Sadness exploded in my chest like a grenade.

Mr Shroff walked over to me. 'Why did you think it was your fault?' he said, frowning.

'Because if I hadn't said anything then we wouldn't be where we were then. If I said no then I would be putting my little brother on the streets and it would be all my fault.'

My hands started to tremble, my legs wanted to buckle.

'But she told me the decision was mine.' I burst into tears.

She should have been there for me, she should never have made me make that choice.

'And what was your decision?' Mr Shroff dug even deeper.

'To let him come back,' I sobbed. I put my hands over my face because I just wanted to hide.

If I could have done a *Doctor Who* and pushed a button to transport myself to another world I would have gone. I was so distressed, I couldn't breathe. David needed help, he was a sick man. But what my mum did was in many ways worse and it's the hardest thing I have had to cope with in my life.

I looked away, with my hands over my face, I couldn't pull myself back from that, I was too upset.

'Lunchtime, Mr Shroff.' The judge came to my rescue, calling for an early lunch.

I was crying so hard I didn't notice everyone leave. The usher opened the box door and I nearly collapsed to the floor. It was like someone had given me oxygen for the first time after I'd been drowning. She pulled me up and I wrapped my arms around my body. If I had been Mr. Tickle from the Mr. Men I would have wrapped them ten times around because I needed to hold myself that badly.

I was still crying when I walked back into the witness room and Jemma jumped up and put her arms around me. We stood there for a moment in silence and then she pulled back, held my shoulders, and looked me right in the eye.

'You're doing so well,' she whispered.

'I need a cigarette, I've got to have a cigarette,' I blurted.

I stood with Mark at the back door, puffing away. I didn't say anything. I didn't feel anything – I was so numb. I just shouted at myself to pull it together because I had to go back in there and carry on. I stamped out my cigarette on the concrete and by the time we walked into the room I'd snapped out of it.

I'm halfway there, half a day done.

'Would any of you like one of my sandwiches?' I asked, opening up the packed lunch I'd prepared that morning.

I suddenly got worried for Mark and Jemma because as much as it was hard for me, it must have been hard for them, too, hearing all that grim detail. I needed to make sure they were OK. They were so special to me because without my friends I would have had no one.

I had my mouth full when I was called to the courtroom again. The usher greeted me differently this time – she wasn't smiling any more, her face looked stony like someone had died.

'You ready to go again?' she asked in a deep and serious voice.

I nodded.

'You are doing so well. You've been brilliant.'

I took that with me as I stepped back into the witness box. Luckily the most painful part was over and I finished giving my evidence for the prosecution. I had a moment to catch my breath and then my stepdad's defence lawyer stepped up. Mr Brown was tall, skinny, he wore glasses and had grey eyebrows to match his barrister's wig. I had him down as being in his late fifties. He walked onto the floor like a cockerel before a fight – his chest puffed out and its feathers splayed.

I was terrified of being cross-examined. If I found it hard for the prosecution, what the hell was this going to be like? Mr Brown went straight for the jugular:

'Can I just make the position clear to you that I do not accept that you ever spoke to your mother about your stepfather sexually abusing you,' he told the courtroom.

'Right,' I said, and frowned.

Idiot.

'So that you know exactly what the case is that I am going to be dealing with, and also that your stepfather never abused you sexually or physically at any time,' he said, and puffed up his chest some more.

'OK,' I said, and shrugged.

That's the best he's got? The lawyer in me came out for the first time.

'I put to you that your stepfather didn't bathe you alone.'

'I put to you' was Mr Brown's favourite phrase.

He tried to trip me up in every way possible. His best line of defence was to attack my memory, because if my dates and detail were inaccurate, then how could the jury believe anything I was saying? I grew angrier by the second.

'Just going back to when you talk about the violence in your childhood, I put it to you, that no one was ever struck around the back of the head with a marble rolling pin, not even you,' he said, and smirked.

Anger ignited in my gut. I threw my shoulders back and put on my lawyer's wig.

'You are making it sound like I stated that it was a volatile relationship and violent all the time. That isn't what I said. I said it *tended* to be. That doesn't mean that it was *all* of the time.'

Take that, Mr Brown.

'So you are saying that there are a lot of bad memories and there were times when your parents were as you describe, volatile, yes?' He cocked his head.

'Yes.'

'But that wasn't all the time?'

'That wasn't all the time,' I repeated sarcastically.

'Well, I certainly suggest to you it was not using weapons like rolling pins.'

Bastard.

'With all due respect, sir, you weren't there,' I fired. As soon as the words left my mouth I regretted it.

'Of course. And you know from your study of law that I have a job to do,' he fired back.

I put my hands over my eyes and took a deep breath.

Calm down, Tina. You're giving a bad impression to the jury. You are going to ruin everything you've done.

'Yes, I know that,' I said.

'So I will carry on doing that.' He cocked his head to the side again.

'Please do,' I said, and smiled. It was my way of an apology.

The judge was quick to step in again and he called an early end to the day at 4.20 p.m. This time I was brave enough to look at the jury as they filed out.

Guy with long black hair and tattoos. I wonder what he does for a living? Girl who looks not a day over sixteen. Would she have felt sorry for me? Chubby man. Guy with big shoulders . . . they all now knew my shameful secret.

'Can you drive? I don't feel strong enough,' I asked Mark, throwing the car keys across the roof.

The heavens opened up as we drove back to Rainham. Jemma and Mark chattered between themselves whilst I leant my head against the window. My cheek smudged up and down as we went over bumps.

My tears were lost in the noise of the rain.

27

Waiting Game

I felt much braver as I walked into the witness box on the second day.

We're nearly done, let's finish this off.

I hadn't slept well but I had too much adrenalin kicking around me to feel tired. Mr Brown started where he had left off but this time I kept my cool. I knew exactly where every question he asked me was leading so I had my answers ready. His only defence was to try to discredit me, but I was too sharp for that. I held my own so well we were finished before lunch.

I could have gone home and rested but there were some people I wanted to see and say thank you to. Sam Aitken (now Sam Shea, I learnt) and Mrs Walsh were both going to be taking the stand after lunch.

'Can you please ask my friend Sam and Mrs Walsh if she will come and see me in the witness room after,' I asked the court usher.

'Of course, love,' she said, and smiled. I could tell she was on my side.

I only had to wait twenty-five minutes before my old best

friend Sam came crashing through the door. Her face was ashen like she'd seen a ghost.

'Fucking hell, I'm pleased as fuck that's fucking over.' She waved her hands in the air. Her language had always been atrocious at the best of times and I burst out laughing.

'Sam, do you realise you just swore three times in one sentence.' I chuckled.

'Oh, my God, that was so terrifying.' She ran her hands through her short blonde hair. She still looked like a tomboy, just twenty years older.

'Are you OK?' I checked.

'Yeah, but thank fuck that's over.'

We sat down on the comfy red chairs and chatted about our schooldays, trying to work out what Mrs Walsh would look like now after all those years.

'I've asked the usher if she would ask Mrs Walsh to come and see me after, but I don't know if she'll want to,' I said to Sam.

'Why wouldn't she?'

'I dunno. Maybe because she wants to put the past behind her now, say her piece and leave,' I said, shrugging.

There was a knock on the door.

'I've got someone here who wants to see you,' said the usher, smiling. Both Sam and I looked at each other like the naughty schoolkids we used to be, about to be told off by the teacher.

It had been twenty years, so I was expecting a weathered sixty-year-old lady to appear. It was like I had used *Doctor Who*'s TARDIS in the end because Mrs Walsh didn't look a day older than when I had known her. Her hair was still neatly parted like a curtain and flicked up at the bottom. Her eyelashes still looked like spiders' legs because they were glued together with thick black mascara.

It felt surreal, as she walked over and greeted me with a warm hug.

'Thank you so much for coming down to give evidence. I really appreciate it,' I said.

Her bottom lip quivered and I saw her vulnerable side for the first time.

'I'm really sorry I failed you.' She lowered her eyes.

I'd promised myself I wouldn't cry again but I couldn't help it.

'You didn't fail me, the school failed me. So don't blame yourself,' I said through my tears.

Sam touched my arm to tell me she was there for me and we all sat down around the coffee table. I dried my eyes and the lawyer in me came out again. I suddenly wanted answers. *Why wasn't I rescued from that house? From that life? Why was I left there to rot?*

'Why did the school never do anything?' I asked my old teacher.

'I don't know,' she said, and shook her head despairingly. 'I followed the procedure, which was to tell the next senior member of staff. I told the deputy head.'

'And she didn't do anything?' I fired.

She lowered her eyes to the ground again.

'Do you remember me giving you a whistle?' she asked.

'No, I don't think I do . . .' I searched my memory but at the time I couldn't receall being given a whistle.

'I gave you a whistle so if he ever came in your bedroom again you could blow it.'

A whistle? What good was a bloody whistle? Why didn't you follow it up? I was at the school for another two years after I told you.

I smiled because I didn't have the energy to tell her what I was really thinking. I was also grateful that she took the stand for me. We talked for a while longer and then she left to return to her life.

'Are you OK?' Sam asked.

'Yeah, I'm just really disappointed.' I bit my lip. I'd cried enough tears to fill a reservoir. I was tired of crying.

I left the court that day feeling exhausted and with a parking ticket. I bought myself the largest bag of Candyking cinema-style sweets on the way home and sat curled up in front of the tele that evening scoffing toffees and fudge and cola bottles.

I tried not to think about the trial or I would have gone insane. I lived in denial over the next few days while my barrister finished his prosecution case. I'd recently started a new job as a carer looking after a lady with a brain injury so my weekend was busy doing night shifts with her.

Monday morning was a different story. That pitted feeling returned to crunch my stomach as I knew my mum and David would be taking to the stand that day for the defence. I imagined her standing there in her T-shirt and calf-length skirt, insisting I'd made the whole thing up. That I was a devil child. I imagined him, with his bald head and sideburns, with a thin film of sweat glistening above his upper lip as he told his pack of lies. Julia Godfrey had asked if I was going to be there to watch them give evidence but I wasn't strong enough to sit in that gallery and listen to them, knowing everything that was coming out of their mouths was lies. Hearing my mum talk like I was nothing would break me. I waited for Julia to tell me how it went instead.

I was pretending to watch TV when the unidentified number flashed up on my phone screen.

'Hi, Julia,' I greeted the child protection officer. It had become a friendship like no other; she knew me so well she could be my best friend but at the same time we weren't friends. I was certain once this was over I'd stay in touch as she'd done so much for me I couldn't thank her enough.

'David Moore has given evidence and so has your mother,' she announced.

'Did my mum get upset?' I had to know.

'No, she came across as quite cold.'

I knew it. She never loved me. Deep breath, don't let it break you, Tina.

'How about David?' I asked.

'David didn't show an ounce of emotion,' she said.

'What nothing? Anger? Sadness?' I gasped.

'Nothing. He hasn't shown any emotion through the whole thing. Not when he was arrested, not when he was interviewed, not when he was charged. He was a bit upset when he talked about his mum dying, but that was it.'

I was speechless. I couldn't get my head around the fact that he didn't show a flicker of guilt for taking my childhood away. There was more:

'I can't go into specific detail but let me tell you, your brothers have done you a favour today, they could almost have been witnesses for the prosecution,' Julia said, and chortled.

'How'd ya mean?'

'Both David and your mum gave evidence to say you never did your washing around their house when you were eighteen years old,' she began explaining.

'OK, yeah,' I said, rolling my eyes at their lies.

'Well, when Jonathan got on the stand, and the barrister asked him if he remembered you coming over to his house, your brother confirmed you used to do your washing at your mum's all the time.'

'Well done, bruv,' I chuckled. Their angelic son had stitched them up. I wasn't being vindictive, I was just happy that finally their lies had caught up with them. A flicker of hope that David Moore would be found guilty by the jury lit in my heart.

'Try to prepare yourself that he might be found not guilty,' said Gayna over a pint on Wednesday night when the jury went out for deliberation.

I couldn't think that way. It was the only thing keeping me going, dreaming he was going to be sent down.

'You'll be so upset if it does go that way and you didn't see it coming,' she coached me.

I stared into my pint.

'Hey, look.' She shook me. 'I'm trying to protect you from any more pain.'

'I know,' I mumbled.

Gayna was right to warn me because the jury didn't come back with a verdict the following day. Or first thing Friday morning like Julia had predicted.

What's taking them so long?

Another hour passed as I waited with Gayna at her house.

He's getting not guilty. They wouldn't be taking so long if they thought he was guilty.

'Do you want another cup of tea?' Gayna got up.

'No, I want to know what the hell is going on, it's lunchtime now,' I snapped. I was watching my mobile on the coffee table like it was a bomb about to go off.

Another half an hour passed.

'I'd wish they would bloody hurry up,' Gayna complained this time. We were on tenterhooks.

'This is killing me, can we just go somewhere please, just so I'm not sitting here waiting for that phone to ring,' I pleaded with my aunt.

'You don't need to ask twice, love.' She picked up her car keys and drove us to the nail salon in Romford.

The nail-varnish fumes made my head spin even more than it was already but it was a welcome distraction. While I was having false nails applied I used my free hand to text Julia – Why is it taking so long?

An unidentified number flashed across the screen.

'I'm really shocked they haven't come back. And they'll be going to lunch soon,' said Julia.

It's not guilty, I know it; the bastard is going to walk away scot-free.

'Please try and stay calm because as soon as I hear something, trust me, you will be the first to know.'

'OK,' I said and hung up.

'Well?' Gayna looked over from her pedicure chair.

'At least another hour because the jury has gone to lunch.'

'Oh, for pity's sake,' Gayna squealed. 'Do you want to get something to eat?'

I wasn't hungry, my stomach was in knots I was so anxious, but I agreed to go to Burger King anyway.

'What's going to happen if they don't reach a verdict today?' Gayna asked as she divvied out our chips and moved the plastic tray on to the spare seat. It was now 2.30 p.m.

'I dunno . . .' I started saying.

An unidentified number flashed across my screen.

'Shit, it's Julia,' I said with a mouth full of food.

'Well, fucking hell, answer it then.' Gayna was on the edge of her seat.

'Hello?'

'Hi, it's Julia.'

'Hiya.'

'Are you on your own?' she asked calmly.

Oh, God, this means it's bad news.

'No, I'm with Gayna.'

'We've got a verdict.'

'Well?'

It was like *The X Factor* when the contestants are kept on tenterhooks waiting for the verdict.

'Guilty.'

'Fuck.'

I burst out in tears as the relief exploded out of me.

'Is that guilty or not guilty?' Gayna screeched because I was so upset she couldn't tell.

'Guilty,' I mouthed to my aunt.

'Gayna, can you get me out of here, I need to get some air,' I gasped, while still on the phone to Julia. We left Burger King but I could barely walk to the car I was so overwhelmed. I could hear Gayna calling everyone she knew.

'There's more,' said Julia.

'What do you mean?' My heart stopped.

'He's also been sentenced today.'

'Already?' I gasped.

'The judge said after watching you go through the trauma of giving evidence he didn't feel there would be any justification for pre-sentencing reports; it wouldn't make any difference.'

'So how long?' I was expecting, one, two, maybe three years. I would have been happy with six months, all I wanted was for him to pay for what he did.

'Fourteen years.'

I stopped dead in the street as the air was whipped out of my lungs.

'Fourteen years,' I whispered to Gayna, shaking in disbelief. My aunt grabbed my arm before my legs buckled. Fourteen years was longer than some murderers get these days. It was amazing. It was justice.

'And when he was sentenced, he showed emotion for the first time!' Julia shouted over my aunt's screams of joy.

'What did he do?'

'As he was being led out David turned to the gallery and called me a fucking cunt,' Julia said, chuckling, clearly happy she'd finally got a rise out of him.

'Ha.' I smiled. I'd destroyed him.

28

Justice

'I can't believe he got fourteen years,' was the saying of the day.

Everyone I rang was as pleased as punch. My boys were so happy for me. I could even hear Dan in the background being upset out of joy as I told Mitchell the good news.

We drove back to Gayna's house and she put the kettle on. I sank into the sofa with an indescribable feeling of relief. All the panic and pain I'd been through for the past eighteen months had been worth it in the end.

'Here you go, love.' Gayna handed me my tea. I hugged it like it was a hot-water bottle. 'I've got an idea, why don't you ring the newspaper? I bet they would be interested to hear your story.' She smirked. She must have hated her sister more than I realised.

I took a slurp of my tea and swirled the idea around in my head.

'OK, hand me the phone.' I held out my hand.

'I'm going to call the *Echo* in Basildon and name and shame the bastard,' I said.

David and Mum lived in Basildon so by putting it in their

local paper everyone in their community would then know what he did to me.

I had the strength of a knight as I dialled the local rag.

'Hello, can I speak to a reporter please?'

Gayna sat next to me on the sofa and craned her ear to the receiver.

''Ello, newsdesk,' a cockney-sounding guy answered.

'I've got a story you might like,' I started.

I proceeded to tell him my story, about the court case; how my stepdad was found guilty of thirteen counts of rape and sexual assault.* I didn't flinch or cry once because I didn't have to be ashamed any more. A jury of twelve peers had believed me.

'Is there a message you want to put out there, Miss Renton? You know, something you've learnt from this?' the reporter asked.

I took a moment and thought about my law degree.

'Yeah, there is actually,' I said. 'To any victims of child abuse, I would say, don't hide. And it doesn't matter how far down the line it is, it's never too late to tell the police.'

'Thanks, Miss Renton. And there's just one more thing . . .'

'Yes?' I arched my eyebrow.

'Under law, I obviously can't identify you in this story as you are a victim of sexual abuse. But would you consider

---

* David Moore was charged with nine counts of sexual assault, four counts of indecent assault on a child and four counts of rape. He was found not guilty of one sexual assault, not guilty of one indecent assault on a child, and one rape charge and one sexual assault charge were dropped.

waving your anonymity? It could help give courage to other women out there who have also suffered, like you.'

I took another moment. Then I really might as well put my face on a billboard in the centre of London. Am I brave enough to do it? Can I cope with everyone looking at me, knowing I've been raped by my stepdad? But it would help other victims.

'OK, let's do it.'

'My full name is Tina Renton,' I said proudly.

I'd got my voice back after years of being forced to stay silent.

Epilogue

'Tina?' said a woman I didn't recognise.

I was standing in Rainham High Street with an arm full of shopping.

'You're Tina, aren't you?' the passer-by persisted.

I panicked that she was someone connected to my mum or brothers, who wanted to hurl abuse at me. I'd heard through the grapevine that Mum, Jonathan and Blake were standing by David, that they visited him in prison.

'Yeah,' I replied hesitantly, picking up my bags to leave.

'I saw you in the paper.' The woman with dark curly hair smiled. She must have been about fifty.

'You're very brave and an inspiration to loads of people.'

My cheeks burnt with embarrassment.

'Oh, thanks, that's very nice of you,' I said coyly.

The woman smiled again and this time her eyes twinkled with kindness. She then walked off down the street. She was just one of many total strangers who have congratulated me for my bravery since the trial. After I gave my name to the local paper, my story went viral and I was headline news in every national paper the following day – EVIL STEPFATHER JAILED 20 YEARS AFTER RAPING GIRL WHO WENT ON TO STUDY LAW.

I have received hundreds of letters of support from all over the world: messages on Facebook and heartfelt emails.

I have been asked to appear on TV chat shows, do radio interviews and star in a documentary about women who have found the courage to speak out about their abuse.

I never expected my story to go so big. I didn't think I was that important. But I guess one of my supporters summed it up perfectly in her letter:

> *Congratulations, Tina! I am so proud of you and the courageous stand you took. By having your step-father arrested for sexual abuse, you showed that help is always available and justice can still prevail. What a role model for victims of abuse! You will make a fine attorney someday.*

The question that everyone asks me is have I finally got closure? And my answer is always the same – I'll never be able to forget the past; that will stay with me for ever. But I've finally found a way to live with it, and be at peace – by getting justice. That horrible anxious feeling has lifted from my stomach. The angry Tina that raged inside me has gone. I want to help other victims of abuse, and if my book saves just one person then I have done my job.

Acknowledgements

This book means so much to me because I needed to be believed. I needed people to know that I am the way I am because I was once a victim, a victim of horrific sexual abuse, at the hands of my mother's husband. I went through the criminal justice system and achieved a better result than I could ever have hoped for. Now I am a survivor, not a victim, and I have many people to thank for getting me where I am today.

First of all I would like to thank Julia Godfrey from the Metropolitan Police for supporting me and for not giving up on building the case to go to court.

I would like to thank the twelve people who sat through the court case listening to the horrible details of what I endured: the jury. You each made the right choice on the evidence that was presented to you by the prosecution. I will NEVER be able to thank each one of you for allowing me the chance to finally gain a little closure on my childhood.

A great big thank you to the witnesses who gave evidence on behalf of the prosecution: for me, without you, this story would not have had a happy ending.

I would like to thank Kerri Sharp, my editor, for giving me the opportunity to tell my story and everyone else at Simon & Schuster for supporting this book.

To my wonderful agent, Rebecca Winfield. I am very

thankful for your professionalism and support. I am so glad we found each other.

To my ghost writer Ruth Kelly, with whom I have spent many days and hours, recounting the details of my life without judgement or criticism. You are now someone I regard as a friend.

I would also like to thank my amazing and wonderful friends for the support and understanding you have offered me throughout my life. I need not mention each of you individually, you know who you are.

I would like to thank filmmaker Richard John Taylor. If our paths had not crossed I do not know where I would be today. I do know you have allowed me the chances and opportunities that 'a girl like me' could only ever have dreamed of. Thank you.

I would like to thank my sons, Mitchell and Daniel, my amazing boys! I am so proud of you and how hard you work to achieve what you want in life. One thing no one can take from me is the unconditional love I feel for my sons, you will both grow to be incredible men.

Endnote

Who would have thought I would be where I am now, working for a company called Princess Films. Richard John Taylor, who set up the company, originally approached me to take part in a documentary about rape. The documentary is called 'I Want to Talk About It' and it will be shown on More4 around Easter 2013. It's a fantastic story about the attitudes of people and the stigma that surrounds rape and sexual abuse. Since filming, Richard and I have become great friends and I am now his PA; who would have thought I would have been clever enough to achieve this.

I would still love to be involved in law or the legal sector, especially as a voice for victims and an advocate for other people who have also been victims of sexual abuse. I am very passionate about fighting for those who have fallen prey to this type of heinous crime, and helping to support them regardless of how long ago the crimes took place. My experience has lead me to believe that my future lies with this career path and hopefully, not too far from now, someone will be able to help me realise my dream – just as I hope I've helped at least one person through their nightmare.

In the meantime I will be always grateful to the people that continue to help me along the way and give me the chance to show I can shine. It's wonderful to know that, regardless of what life has thrown at me, there will be some good to come out of it by the end!

One thing I do know for sure is that if you have been a victim in any way, regardless of whether it was yesterday or twenty years ago, you don't have to suffer in silence. There are support groups that can help you or members of your family. There is help out there, believe me, and I have included just a few links below. Many more can be found through an online search engine.

www.aftersilence.org

www.rapecrisis.org.uk

www.dancinginthedarkness.com

Finally, I would like to say thank you to each and every one of you who has taken the time to read my story. Whether you are a professional working in this sector or someone personally affected by this type of crime, I hope my story will help you to move on with your future.

If you wish to contact me you can do so by email:

tinarenton@gmail.com